# KitchenAid®

# Best-Loved Recipes

Publications International, Ltd.

Favorite Brand Name Recipes at www.fbnr.com

**Photography** on pages 16, 23, 25, 27, 38, 43, 45, 62, 67, 84, 89, 91, 93, 99, 106, 111, 126, 131, 133, 144, 147, 149, 151, 153, 174, 179, 196, 218, 228, and 233 by Stephen Hamilton Photographics, Inc.

**Pictured on the front cover:** Chocolate Frosting *(page 101)*.
**Pictured on the back cover** *(left to right)*: Vegetarian Sushi Maki *(page 18)*, Crunchy Whole Grain Bread *(page 40)*, and Marble Cheesecake *(page 92)*.

**Microwave Cooking:** Microwave ovens vary in wattage. Use the cooking times as guidelines and check for doneness before adding more time.

# contents

# The KitchenAid® Stand Mixer:
# Ninety Years of Quality

Since KitchenAid first brought amazing convenience to American kitchens 90 years ago, cooks have enjoyed using our products to mix up their own delicious innovations. From *Crunchy Whole Grain Bread* to *Rustic Dried Cherry Salad*, **KitchenAid® Best-Loved Recipes** encompasses a tantalizing array of dishes that are sure to delight your senses and please your palate. We hope you'll find the past interesting and the future taste-tempting as you try our exciting appetizers, main courses, breads, and desserts.

A Humble Beginning

The history of the iconic KitchenAid stand mixer began with a chance encounter between an overburdened baker and an industrious engineer. The year was 1908, and Herbert Johnston, an engineer at the Hobart Manufacturing Company in Troy, Ohio, was watching the baker mix bread dough with an age-old iron spoon. Convinced there had to be a better way, Johnston set to work developing an 80-quart electric stand mixer. Less than seven years later, professional bakers across the country had

## KITCHENAID APPLIANCE HISTORY TIME LINE

The history of KitchenAid appliances can be said to parallel the history of advancing technology in the United States. The origins of the company are more than a century old, rooted primarily in two inventions—the dishwasher and the stand mixer—that were conceived 25 years apart in two small Midwestern towns.

### 1883

Socialite Josephine Cochrane of Shelbyville, Illinois, is determined to invent a mechanical way of cleaning dishes, so she experiments with spraying hot, soapy water on plates. Three years later, the Garis-Cochrane Manufacturing Company (whose name was chosen to hide that its president was a woman) is issued the first of several patents for her commercial dishwasher. Twenty years later, she develops a home model.

### 1908

Engineer Herbert Johnston sees a baker mix bread dough with a heavy iron spoon. Convinced there has to be a better way, he begins designing the first commercial stand mixer.

an easier and more efficient way of getting the job done.

The amazing new labor-saving machine caught on so quickly, the U.S. Navy ordered stand mixers for its three new battleships: the *California*, the *Tennessee*, and the *South Carolina*. By 1917, the stand mixer was classified as "regular equipment" on all U.S. Navy ships. The product's overwhelming success prompted Hobart engineers to design a smaller model that could be used in home kitchens. But World War I interfered, and the concept would have to wait until peacetime returned.

1919: The Birth of Unprecedented Quality
The year 1919 was truly a time of change. The gray days of war were giving way to the gaiety of the Roaring '20s, and an era of prosperity and progress was upon us. Like other war munitions plants across the country, the Troy Metal Products Company (a subsidiary of Hobart), revived its peacetime

## 1914  1919  1920  1923  1926

The Model H-5, the first stand mixer for the home, is introduced. Called "the best kitchen aid" by an executive's wife, a brand is born, and the KitchenAid trademark is registered with the U.S. Patent Office.

The Model H-5 offers attachments that do everything from slicing to straining, branding KitchenAid stand mixers as versatile "food preparation tools." Today's KitchenAid stand mixers can be converted to various kitchen tools such as a pasta maker, sausage stuffer, food grinder, citrus juicer, and ice cream maker via more than a dozen optional attachments.

Interestingly, all stand mixer attachments will fit any KitchenAid stand mixer, including the original.

KitchenAid launches an advertising campaign for its home stand mixer in the national media.

KitchenAid acquires the Crescent Washing Machine (one of the names used for Josephine Cochrane's design after her death) and changes the name to Warewasher.

The Model H, an 80-quart capacity commercial stand mixer designed by Johnston, hits the market. Within three years, it is specified as standard equipment on all U.S. Navy ships.

The KitchenAid Manufacturing Company is created. KitchenAid stand mixer operations move to Troy, Ohio.

efforts, and set to work on the Model H-5 stand mixer— the first electric "food preparer" for the home.

Wives of Troy executives were commissioned to test the initial prototypes. After a successful trial run, one famously reported, "I don't care what you call it, but I know it's the best kitchen aid I have ever had!" A brand name was born, and the first KitchenAid stand mixer was unveiled to the American consumer in 1919. The H-5 was the first in a long line of KitchenAid stand mixers that utilized "planetary action," a revolutionary design that rotated the beater in one direction while moving it around the bowl in the opposite path, and included time-saving attachments such as a food grinder and a juicer.

## KITCHENAID APPLIANCE HISTORY TIME LINE

| 1927 | 1935 | 1936 | 1937 | 1941 | 1942 |

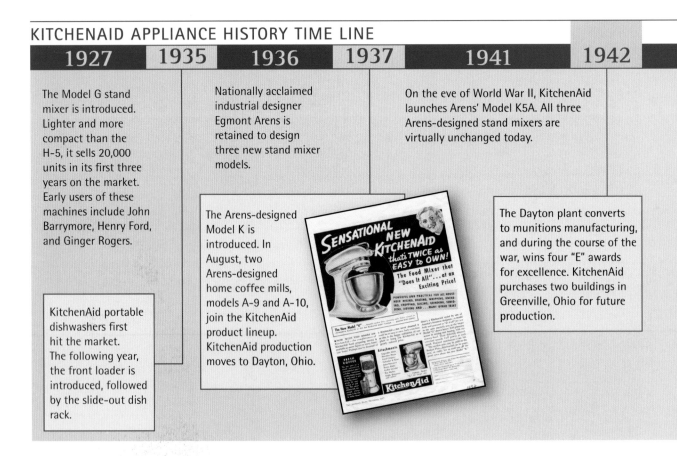

**1927**

The Model G stand mixer is introduced. Lighter and more compact than the H-5, it sells 20,000 units in its first three years on the market. Early users of these machines include John Barrymore, Henry Ford, and Ginger Rogers.

KitchenAid portable dishwashers first hit the market. The following year, the front loader is introduced, followed by the slide-out dish rack.

**1935**

Nationally acclaimed industrial designer Egmont Arens is retained to design three new stand mixer models.

**1936**

The Arens-designed Model K is introduced. In August, two Arens-designed home coffee mills, models A-9 and A-10, join the KitchenAid product lineup. KitchenAid production moves to Dayton, Ohio.

**1937**

On the eve of World War II, KitchenAid launches Arens' Model K5A. All three Arens-designed stand mixers are virtually unchanged today.

**1942**

The Dayton plant converts to munitions manufacturing, and during the course of the war, wins four "E" awards for excellence. KitchenAid purchases two buildings in Greenville, Ohio for future production.

The new stand mixer rolled off the assembly line at the rate of four per day, but retailers were initially hesitant to carry the unique product. Undeterred, the company's largely female sales force set out to sell the 65-pound H-5 door to door. They gave in-home demonstrations to groups of modern women looking to simplify their lives with an exciting new machine that could mix, beat, cut, cream, slice, chop, grind, strain, and freeze.

Innovation and quality have always been the hallmark of KitchenAid appliances, and as the decades wore on, the company focused on meeting consumer's changing needs. When urbanization brought Americans into smaller city dwellings, KitchenAid responded with the Model G, a less

## 1946

The end of World War II sees the resumption of peacetime production, which is moved from Dayton to Greenville, Ohio.

KitchenAid introduces the KD-10 dishwasher designed for home use. Unlike other residential dishwashers that simply splash water on dishes, it distributes water through a pressurized system.

## 1955

## 1962

The 4½-quart-capacity Model K45 is introduced. The most popular KitchenAid stand mixer ever, the K45 is still an important model in the line.

KitchenAid enters the cooking business by purchasing the Chambers Range Company, which was founded in 1912 in Shelbyville, Indiana.

KitchenAid unveils stylish new stand mixer colors at the Atlantic City Housewares Show. Colors include Petal Pink, Sunny Yellow, Island Green, Satin Chrome, and Antique Copper.

## 1970

Harvest Wheat and Avocado are added to the list of available stand mixer colors.

## 1986

KitchenAid offers a complete suite of large appliances for the kitchen by adding a refrigerator to their growing product lineup.

KitchenAid blenders join the KitchenAid line of portable appliances.

## 1992

expensive, more compact version of the H-5 that weighed half as much. As the country experienced economic downturn in the 1930s, the company recruited renowned industrial designer Egmont Arens to design three new, more affordable stand mixer models. Arens' designs held such timeless simplicity and function that they remain virtually unchanged to this day.

By the late 1930s, demand for KitchenAid stand mixers was so great that the factory sold out before Christmas each year. But in 1941, war again intervened, and the plant limited its production of stand mixers to focus on munitions. Regular manufacturing resumed in 1946, and to expand its production capabilities, KitchenAid moved to Greenville, Ohio, where dedicated employees continue to proudly produce the KitchenAid stand mixer today.

Since 1919, the KitchenAid brand has brought unprecedented

## KITCHENAID APPLIANCE HISTORY TIME LINE

| 1993 | 1994 | 1998 | 1999 | 2000 | 2001 |
|------|------|------|------|------|------|

**1993** — Food processor models are added to the line.

**1998** — KitchenAid announces the Architect® Series, a suite of stainless steel appliances that includes the first stainless steel dishwasher exteriors. With features inspired by, and created for, those who love to cook and entertain, the design of each piece complements each other for a complete kitchen suite.

**1994** — KitchenAid announces the construction of a new world-class 185,000-square-foot plant in Greenville, Ohio.

KitchenAid debuts suites of countertop appliances in matching bold colors such as Empire Red and Cobalt Blue.

**1999** — KitchenAid focuses on the home chef and launches lines of cookware, bakeware, cutlery, kitchen textiles, and other products.

**2000** — Expanding its line of premium food processors, KitchenAid introduces a new 11-cup, three-bowl food processor with a citrus press.

The new Professional 6™ stand mixer is introduced, offering greater capacity to give home bakers the ability to mix dough for multiple loaves of breads, cakes, and cookies all at one time.

**2001** — KitchenAid announces fully integrated dishwashers with concealed controls and a choice of color, stainless steel, or customized panel-ready doors.

Cook for the Cure®, a partnership between KitchenAid and Susan G. Komen for the Cure, is born. Money is initially raised for breast cancer research and education through the sale of the pink stand mixer, though additional philanthropic initiatives are later added.

convenience and ingenuity into kitchens across the globe. From pioneering planetary action 90 years ago to unveiling the first stand mixers in Petal Pink, Sunny Yellow, and other stylish colors in 1955, our products have been at the forefront of culinary trends. Today, the KitchenAid legacy of quality lives on not only in the multifunctional stand mixer and its attachments, but also in the full line of kitchen appliances, gadgets and utensils, cookware, bakeware, cutlery, and kitchen textiles sold around the world. Every product that carries the KitchenAid name, whether purchased in Paris or Peoria, is guaranteed to be strong, reliable, versatile, and backed by more than 90 years of quality and excellence.

## 2002 | 2003 | 2004 | 2005 | 2007 | 2009

In conjunction with the International Association of Culinary Professionals (IACP), and supported by culinary notables, including the late Julia Child, KitchenAid is a founding member of Endangered Treasures, a program dedicated to preserving and restoring historic cookbooks, menus, and other materials.

Convection ovens are added to the cooking product lineup.

Briva®, KitchenAid brand's breakthrough in-sink dishwasher, becomes available for homes with standard-sized cabinetry.

KitchenAid unveils a two-drawer dishwasher, which is capable of washing two loads simultaneously at completely different cycle settings.

KitchenAid introduces the first full-size range with steam assist cooking.

An evolution from the successful first generation of suite appliances, Architect® Series II is introduced.

To date, KitchenAid has raised more than $6 million for Susan G. Komen for the Cure with a variety of Cook for the Cure programs including: the sales of their limited-edition pink products, which generate a donation with each purchase and registration; auctions at KitchenAid-sponsored culinary events; and educating people how to host parties at home that raise funds to help fight breast cancer.

COOK FOR THE CURE
PRESENTED BY
KitchenAid

# Glossary of Cooking Terms

**Al Dente:** The literal translation of this Italian phrase is "to the tooth." It indicates a degree of doneness when cooking pasta. Al dente pasta is slightly firm and chewy, rather than soft.

**Baste:** Basting is the technique of brushing, spooning, or pouring liquids over food—usually meat and poultry—as it cooks. Basting helps preserve moistness, adds flavor, and gives foods an attractive appearance. Melted butter, pan drippings, broth, or a combination of these ingredients are frequently used. Sometimes seasonings or flavorings are added.

**Beat:** Beating is the technique of stirring or mixing vigorously. Beating introduces air into egg whites, egg yolks, and whipping cream; mixes two or more ingredients to form a homogeneous mixture; or makes a mixture smoother, lighter, and creamier. Beating can be done with a variety of tools, including a spoon, fork, wire whisk, rotary eggbeater, or electric mixer.

**Blanch:** Blanching means cooking foods, most often vegetables, briefly in boiling water and then quickly cooling them in cold water. Food is blanched for one or more of the following reasons: to loosen and remove skin (tomatoes, peaches, almonds); to enhance color and reduce bitterness (raw vegetables for crudités); and to extend storage life (raw vegetables to be frozen).

**Blend:** Blending is the technique of mixing together two or more ingredients until they are thoroughly combined. The ingredients may be blended together with an electric mixer or electric blender, or by hand using a wooden spoon or wire whisk.

**Boil:** To bring to a boil means to heat a liquid until bubbles break the surface. Boiling refers to cooking food in boiling water. For a "full rolling boil," bubbles break the surface continuously and cannot be stirred away.

**Braise:** Braising is a moist-heat cooking method used to tenderize tough cuts of meat or fibrous vegetables. Food is first browned in fat and then gently simmered in a small amount of liquid in a tightly covered skillet until tender. This can be done on the rangetop or in the oven. The liquid—such as water, broth, wine, or beer—often has finely chopped vegetables and herbs added for flavor.

**Broil:** Broiling is the technique of cooking foods a measured distance from a direct source of heat. Both gas and electric ovens provide a means of broiling. Some rangetops have built-in grills that provide another broiling option. Grilling on a barbecue grill also fits this broad definition of broiling. The goal of broiling is to brown the exterior without overcooking the interior. Generally, the thinner the food item, the closer it should be to the heat source.

Brush: Brushing refers to the technique of applying a liquid such as melted butter, barbecue sauce, or glaze to the surface of food prior to or during cooking with a brush. It serves the same purpose as basting: preserving moistness, adding flavor, and giving foods an attractive appearance.

Caramelize: Caramelizing is the technique of cooking sugar, sometimes with a small amount of water, to a very high temperature (between 310°F and 360°F) so that it melts into a clear brown liquid and develops a characteristic flavor. The color can vary from light golden brown to dark brown. Caramelized sugar, sometimes called "burnt sugar," is used in a variety of desserts and sauces.

Chill: Chilling is the technique of cooling foods, usually in the refrigerator or over ice, to a temperature of 35°F to 40°F. A recipe or dish may require several hours or as long as overnight to chill thoroughly. To chill a large portion of a hot mixture such as soup or chili, separate the mixture into several small containers for quicker cooling. To chill small amounts of hot food, place the food in a bowl or saucepan over a container of crushed ice or iced water, or chill the food in the freezer for 20 to 30 minutes.

Chop: Chopping is the technique of cutting food into small, irregularly shaped pieces. Although the term does not designate a specific size, most cooks would suggest that food be chopped into approximately 1/4-inch pieces. Chopped food is larger than minced food and more irregularly cut than diced food. Recipe directions may call for a coarsely chopped or a finely chopped ingredient.

Coat: To coat means to cover food with an outer layer, usually fine or powdery, using ingredients such as flour, crumbs, cornmeal, or sugar. With foods such as chicken, fish fillets, and eggplant, this coating is preliminary to frying or baking and provides a crispy exterior. Such foods are often first rolled in eggs or milk so the coating adheres. Some cookies are coated with sugar before or after baking.

Combine: Combining is the process of mixing two or more liquid or dry ingredients together to make them a uniform mixture.

Core: Coring means to remove the center seed-bearing structure of a fruit or vegetable. The most commonly cored foods are apples, pears, pineapple, zucchini, and cucumbers. First cutting the food into quarters and then cutting out the center core can accomplish coring with a small knife. A utensil specially designed to remove the core of specific whole fruits and vegetables is known as a corer. The most common corers are for apples, pears, and pineapple.

Crumble: To crumble means to break food into small pieces of irregular size. It is usually done with the fingers. Ingredients often crumbled include blue cheese and bacon. Both foods can be purchased in the supermarket already crumbled.

**Crush:** Crushing means reducing a food, such as crackers, to small fine particles by rolling with a rolling pin or pounding with a mortar and pestle. A food processor or blender also works well. Fruit can be crushed to extract its juices. Garlic is sometimes crushed with the flat side of a knife blade or garlic press to release its flavor.

**Cutting In:** Cutting in is the technique used to combine a chilled solid fat such as shortening or butter with dry ingredients such as flour, so that the resulting mixture is in coarse, small pieces. A fork, two table knives, fingers, or a pastry blender may be used. If using a food processor, be careful not to overmix the ingredients. This process is used to make biscuits, scones, pie pastry, and some cookies.

**Deglaze:** Deglazing is the technique used to retrieve the flavorful bits that adhere to a pan after a food, usually meat, has been browned and the excess fat has been drained. While the pan is still hot, a small amount of liquid (water, wine, or broth) is added and stirred to loosen the browned bits in the pan. The resulting liquid is used as a base for sauces and gravies.

**Degrease:** Degreasing is a technique used to remove fat from the surface of a liquid such as soup or broth. It can be accomplished in several ways. First remove the soup or broth from the heat and allow it to stand briefly until the fat rises. The quickest degreasing method is to skim off the fat using a large spoon. If the fat to be removed is animal fat, the liquid may be chilled; the animal fat will harden, making it easy to lift off.

**Dice:** To dice is to cut food into small cubes that are uniform in size. The smallest dice, which is about $1/8$ of an inch, is best suited for delicate garnishing. More typical are sizes between $1/4$ and $1/2$ of an inch. Dicing is distinguished from chopping and mincing by the care taken to achieve a uniform size for an attractive presentation.

**Dot:** This term, generally used in cooking as "to dot with butter," refers to cutting butter into small bits and scattering them over a food. This technique allows the butter to melt evenly. It also keeps the food moist, adds richness, and can promote browning.

**Dust:** Dusting is a technique used to lightly coat a food, before or after cooking, with a powdery ingredient such as flour or powdered sugar. The ingredient may be sprinkled on using your fingers or shaken from a small sieve or a container with holes on the top. A greased baking pan can be dusted with flour before it is filled, a technique also known as "flouring."

**Flake:** To flake refers to the technique of separating or breaking off small pieces or layers of a food using a utensil, such as a fork. For example, cooked fish fillets may be flaked for use in a salad or main dish.

**Glossary of Cooking Terms**

**Flour:** To flour means to apply a light coating of flour to a food or piece of equipment. Applied to food, the flour dries the surface. This helps food brown better when frying and keeps food such as raisins from sticking together. Baking pans are floured for better release characteristics and to produce thin, crisp crusts. Rolling pins, biscuit cutters, cookie cutters, and work surfaces are floured to prevent doughs from sticking to them.

**Fold:** Folding is a specialized technique for combining two ingredients or mixtures, one of which usually has been aerated, such as whipped cream or egg whites. It is best done by placing the airy mixture on top of the other and, with a rubber spatula, gently but quickly cutting through to the bottom and turning the ingredients over with a rolling motion. The bowl is rotated a quarter-turn each time and the process repeated until the mixtures are combined with as little loss in volume as possible. Care must be taken not to stir, beat, or overmix. Fruit pieces, chips, or nuts may be folded into an airy mixture using the same technique.

**Fry:** Frying refers to the technique of cooking foods in hot fat, usually vegetable oil. Proper fat temperature is critical to a successful result. The ideal temperature produces a crisp exterior and a moist, perfectly cooked interior; too high a temperature will burn the food, and too low a temperature will result in food absorbing excessive fat. A deep-fat thermometer is essential to determining the temperature of the fat. Deep-fried foods are submerged or floated in hot fat in a large heavy saucepan or Dutch oven. Electric deep fryers fitted with wire baskets are available. Pan-frying refers to cooking food in a skillet in a small amount of fat that does not cover the food.

**Grate:** Grating refers is the technique of making very small particles from a firm food like carrots, lemon peel, or Parmesan cheese by rubbing it along a coarse surface with small, sharp protrusions, usually a metal kitchen grater. Food may also be grated in a food processor using a specialized metal blade.

**Knead:** Kneading refers to the technique of manipulating bread dough in order to develop the protein in flour, called gluten, to ensure the structure of the finished product. Kneading also aids in combining the dough ingredients. Biscuit dough is lightly kneaded—only about ten times—whereas yeast doughs may be vigorously kneaded for several minutes.

**Mash:** To mash is to crush a food into a soft, smooth mixture, as in mashed potatoes or bananas. It can be done with a tool called a potato masher or with an electric mixer. Small amounts of food, such as one or two bananas or a few hard-cooked egg yolks, can be mashed with a fork. For best results with potatoes, make sure they are fully cooked so they are soft enough to become completely smooth.

**Mince:** Mincing refers to the technique of chopping food into very tiny, irregular pieces. Minced food is smaller than chopped food. Flavorful seasonings, such as garlic and fresh herbs, are often minced to distribute their flavor more evenly throughout a dish.

**Purée:** To purée means to mash or strain a soft or cooked food until it has a smooth consistency. This can be done with a food processor, sieve, blender, or food mill. For best results, the food must be naturally soft, such as raspberries or ripe pears, or cooked until it is completely tender. Puréed foods are used as sauces and as ingredients in other sweet or savory dishes. The term also refers to the foods that result from the process.

**Reduce:** To reduce is to boil a liquid, usually a sauce, until its volume has been decreased through evaporation. This results in a more intense flavor and thicker consistency. Typically, reduced sauces are one-third or one-half of their original volume. Use a pan with a wide bottom to shorten preparation time. The reduced product is referred to as a "reduction." Since the flavor of any seasonings would also become concentrated when a sauce is reduced, add the seasonings to the sauce after it has been reduced.

**Roast:** Roasting involves cooking poultry and large tender cuts of meat in the oven in an uncovered pan. Roasting produces a nicely browned exterior and a moist interior. Roasting vegetables intensifies their natural sweetness. Vegetables such as onions and carrots can be roasted alongside meat. Many vegetables can be roasted and served as a side dish or used as ingredients in other dishes.

**Roll Out:** To roll out means to flatten dough into an even layer using a rolling pin. To roll out pastry or cookie dough, place the dough—which should be in the shape of a disc—on a floured surface, such as a counter, pastry cloth, or a large cutting board. Lightly flour your hands and the rolling pin. Place the rolling pin across the center of the dough. With several light strokes, roll the rolling pin away from you toward the edge of the dough. Turn the dough a quarter-turn and roll again from the center to the edge. Repeat this process until the dough is the desired thickness. If the dough becomes sticky, dust it and the rolling pin with flour. If the dough sticks to the surface, gently fold back the edge of the dough and dust the surface underneath the dough with flour.

**Sauté:** Sautéing is the technique of rapidly cooking or browning food in a small amount of fat in a skillet or sauté pan. The food is constantly stirred, turned, or tossed to keep it from sticking or burning. Thin, tender cuts of meat—such as steaks, lamb chops, sliced pork tenderloin, flattened chicken breasts, and fish fillets—are candidates for sautéing. The objective is to brown the food on the outside in the time needed to cook the interior. This requires medium-high heat. Oil can withstand the higher heat needed for sautéing. For flavor, a little butter can be added to the oil, but do not use only butter because it will burn before the food browns.

Sift: Sifting is the technique of passing a dry ingredient such as flour or powdered sugar through the fine mesh of a sieve or sifter for the purpose of breaking up lumps and making it lighter in texture. Sifting results in lighter baked goods and smoother frostings. Most all-purpose flour is presifted, but many bakers sift even presifted flour to achieve a fine, light texture. Cake flour is generally sifted before using. Spoon the ingredient into the sieve and push it through the mesh screen using a metal spoon or rubber spatula.

Simmer: To simmer is to cook a liquid or a food in a liquid with gentle heat just below the boiling point. Small bubbles slowly rising to the surface of the liquid indicate simmering.

Sliver: To sliver is the technique of cutting food into thin strips or pieces. Basil and garlic are two ingredients that may be identified as slivered in a recipe.

Steam: Steaming is a method of cooking food, usually vegetables, in the steam given off by boiling water. The food is held above, but not in, the boiling or simmering water in a covered pan. The steam swirls around the food and cooks it with an intense, moist heat. Steaming helps to retain flavor, color, shape, texture, and many of the vitamins and minerals. Steaming is often done in a two-pan steamer, a steamer basket, or a bamboo steamer.

Strain: Straining refers to the technique of pouring a liquid through the small holes of a strainer or the wire mesh of a sieve to remove lumps or unwanted particles.

Toast: Toasting is the technique of browning foods by means of dry heat. Bread products, nuts, seeds, and coconut are commonly toasted. Toasting is done in a toaster, toaster oven, oven, or skillet, or under the broiler. The purpose of toasting bread is to brown, crisp, and dry it. Nuts, seeds, and coconut are toasted to intensify their flavor.

Whip: To whip refers to the technique of beating ingredients such as egg whites and whipping cream with a wire whisk or electric mixer in order to incorporate air and increase their volume. This results in a light, fluffy texture.

Whisk: Whisking is the technique of stirring, beating, or whipping foods with a wire whisk. If you do not have a whisk, you can use a wooden spoon if the purpose is to blend ingredients. For whipping foods, an electric mixer can be used instead.

Vegetarian Sushi Maki *(recipe on page 18)*

# appetizers

Whether cooking for company or adding
a touch of elegance to an otherwise casual
family dinner, this collection of appetizers
is surprisingly simple to create, yet
undeniably inspiring to the palate.

From sushi to Samosas and cream puffs
to crostini, these little bites are the perfect
prelude to a divine dining experience.

# Vegetarian Sushi Maki

*(photo on page 16)*

4 to 6 sheets toasted sushi
    nori

1 teaspoon wasabi or prepared
    mustard

1½ cups cooked Sushi Rice*
    (recipe follows)

1 ripe avocado, thinly sliced

4 thin strips peeled cucumber

1 handful spinach leaves,
    thinly sliced

½ cup steamed and thinly
    sliced carrot

4 teaspoons toasted sesame
    seeds

12 thin slivers pickled ginger

1 to 2 tablespoons soy sauce

*Sushi rice can often be found in the Asian
foods aisle in well-stocked grocery stores. For
sushi with a chewier texture, try substituting
brown rice.*

*Makes 6 to 8 rolls*

1 Place 1 sheet of nori on flat work surface. Cover bottom third of sheet
with thin layer of wasabi. Spread about ⅓ cup rice on top of wasabi,
leaving an inch uncovered along bottom edge. Distribute one-fourth of
each of remaining ingredients on top of rice.

2 Wet middle fingers with water. Moisten top edge of nori sheet. Lift
bottom edge and press it into rice, rolling rice into nori as you would
a jellyroll, until it is folded over to top edge. Press gently to seal. Store in
cool place up to 6 hours.

3 Cut rolls into 1-inch slices with sharp knife, wiping knife with warm
water if it gets sticky. Place rolls decoratively on a platter, cut side up.
Serve with pickled ginger and soy sauce.

## Sushi Rice

*Makes 2 cups*

1¾ **cups water**

½ **teaspoon salt**

1 **cup short-grain brown rice or sushi rice**

⅓ **cup rice vinegar**

1 **tablespoon sugar**

1 **teaspoon salt**

Bring water and salt to a boil in small saucepan. Add rice; stir and
reduce heat to simmer. Simmer, covered, 40 minutes for brown rice or 20
minutes for sushi rice.

Remove from heat; let stand 5 minutes.

Remove rice from pot; let cool slightly.

While still warm, combine rice with vinegar, sugar and salt. Stir gently.

# Margherita Panini Bites

1 loaf (16 ounces) ciabatta
  or crusty Italian bread, cut
  into 16 (½-inch) slices
8 teaspoons Pesto Sauce
  (see recipe on page 195)
16 fresh basil leaves
8 slices mozzarella cheese
24 thin slices Roma tomatoes
  (about 2 large tomatoes)
  Olive oil

*Makes 32 panini bites*

1 Spread 8 slices of bread with 1 teaspoon pesto each. Top each slice with 2 basil leaves, 1 slice mozzarella cheese and 3 tomato slices. Top with remaining slices of bread.

2 Brush both sides of sandwiches lightly with olive oil. Grill sandwiches in stovetop grill pan, indoor grill or in skillet until lightly browned.

3 Cut each sandwich into 4 pieces.
Serve warm.

# Asian Barbecue Skewers

2 pounds boneless, skinless chicken thighs

1/2 cup soy sauce

1/3 cup packed brown sugar

2 tablespoons sesame oil

3 cloves garlic, minced

1/2 cup thinly sliced green onions

1 tablespoon toasted sesame seeds (optional)

*Makes 4 to 6 servings*

1 Cut each thigh into 4 pieces about 1 1/2 inches thick. Thread chicken onto 7-inch-long wooden skewers, folding thinner pieces, if necessary. Place skewers in 7-quart slow cooker, layering as flat as possible.

2 Combine soy sauce, brown sugar, oil and garlic in small bowl. Reserve 1/3 cup sauce; set aside. Pour remaining sauce over skewers. Cover; cook on LOW 2 hours. Turn skewers over and cook 1 hour longer.

3 Transfer skewers to serving platter. Discard cooking liquid. Spoon on reserved sauce and sprinkle with sliced green onions and sesame seeds, if desired.

# Prosciutto-Wrapped Figs with Orange-Honey Sauce

16 dried mission figs

8 slices prosciutto

6 tablespoons orange juice

1 tablespoon honey

2 teaspoons freshly squeezed lemon juice

Red pepper flakes

Salt (optional)

*Makes 8 servings*

1 Place figs in small saucepan; cover with water. Bring to a boil over medium-high heat. Reduce heat; cover and simmer 8 minutes or until figs are soft. Drain and set aside to cool.

2 Meanwhile, cut prosciutto slices in half lengthwise. Wrap each fig with prosciutto strip; secure with toothpick. Arrange on serving plate.

3 Combine orange juice, honey, lemon juice, red pepper flakes and salt, if desired, in small saucepan. Bring to a boil over medium-high heat. Cook 2 minutes or until mixture is syrupy and reduced by half. Drizzle sauce over figs or serve on side for dipping.

Asian Barbecue Skewers

# Arancini

4 servings Risotto alla
    Milanese (recipe follows)

12 (½-inch) slices fresh
    mozzarella

12 (½-inch) slices fresh
    Parmigiano Reggiano
    cheese

12 (¼-inch) cubes ham

3 egg whites, beaten

1½ cups dry Italian bread
    crumbs

2 cups canola oil

## TIP

*Arancini, which literally means "little orange" in Italian, is a popular Sicilian dish made of fried rice balls. Arancini are often filled with cheeses or meats and are the perfect appetizer for a cocktail party or holiday gathering.*

*Makes 12 small arancini*

1. Prepare 1 recipe Risotto alla Milanese. Spread on platter or sheet tray to cool.

2. Spoon 2 tablespoons of cooled risotto into palm. Flatten risotto into 3×3-inch disk. Place 1 piece each mozzarella, Parmigiano and ham into center of each disk.

3. Fold disk into ball. Gently pinch edges of ball together around filling. Roll ball between palms to roughly the size of a large egg. Dip ball in bread crumbs, then egg whites and again in breadcrumbs. Set on tray. Repeat until all risotto is used.

4. Place tray in refrigerator and chill at least 1 hour, or up to overnight, covered with plastic wrap.

5. Heat oil in deep frying pan to 360°F. Place each rice ball in hot oil. Fry until golden brown, about 1 minute on each side. Remove with slotted spoon and place on wire rack. Serve warm.

## Risotto alla Milanese

*Makes 4 servings*

  2 tablespoons olive oil

  2 tablespoons butter

  1 shallot, minced

  ¼ cup white wine

  1 generous pinch saffron threads, ground to a powder in a mortar

  1 cup arborio rice

  4 cups chicken or vegetable broth, heated to just under a boil

  ¼ cup grated Parmesan cheese

    Black pepper

Heat olive oil in deep saucepan over medium-high heat; add butter. When butter has melted, add shallot. Cook and stir 30 to 45 seconds or until just beginning to brown.

Add wine; stir constantly until wine evaporates. Add saffron and mix well.

Add arborio rice; stir until rice is completely coated with olive oil/butter mixture. Cook 1 to 2 minutes or until edges of rice become translucent.

Reduce heat to medium-low and add ½ cup of hot stock, stirring constantly until rice absorbs all of stock.

Add another ½ cup of stock; stir constantly until absorbed. Repeat until all stock is used. Add cheese and pepper to taste.

# Pakoras

4 cups canola oil

1½ cups Besan (recipe follows)

1 teaspoon baking soda

2 teaspoons salt

½ teaspoon turmeric

½ teaspoon chili powder

¼ teaspoon garlic powder

½ cup water mixed with ¼ cup plain yogurt

1 large zucchini, stemmed and sliced into ¼-inch rounds

1 medium sweet potato, sliced into ¼-inch rounds

½ small butternut squash, peeled, seeded and sliced into ¼-inch-thick pieces

1 small Asian eggplant, stemmed and sliced into ¼-inch rounds

¼ cup water

Tamarind Sauce
(see recipe on page 27)

*Makes 4 to 6 servings*

1 Heat oil in deep saucepan until it reaches 350°F. Meanwhile, mix Besan, baking soda, salt, turmeric, chili and garlic powders in bowl of electric stand mixer until thoroughly combined, 5 to 10 seconds. Add enough of water/yogurt mixture to create thick batter similar to pancake batter; stir to combine.

2 Place vegetable slices in microwaveable bowl with water. Cover with plastic wrap; microwave on HIGH 2 minutes. Remove from microwave; set aside to cool. Drain water and pat dry with paper towels.

3 Dip vegetable slices into batter and coat well. Carefully place in oil. Fry until golden brown, about 30 seconds per side.

4 Remove vegetable slices from oil and place on wire rack. Serve warm with Tamarind Sauce.

## Besan

**1 pound dry chickpeas**

Preheat oven to 350°F. Place chickpeas on sheet tray and bake until just golden brown, 5 to 10 minutes. Alternatively, place chickpeas in large, flat skillet on stovetop over medium heat. Cook and stir often until just golden brown, 5 to 7 minutes.

Remove chickpeas from heat; allow to cool completely. Place in food processor with metal blade. Pulse until coarse meal forms.

Process until smooth powder is created.

# Samosas

2¼ cups plus 3 tablespoons
   all-purpose flour, divided

½ teaspoon salt

4 tablespoons plus 3 to 4 cups
   vegetable oil, divided

2 large potatoes, peeled

1 bunch green onions, trimmed
   and chopped

2 fresh green chilies, seeded
   and minced (optional)*

½ cup chopped fresh cilantro

1 teaspoon whole cumin seeds

2 teaspoons curry powder

½ teaspoon salt

   Tamarind Sauce
   (recipe follows)

*Jalapeño peppers can sting and irritate the skin, so wear rubber gloves when handling peppers and do not touch your eyes.*

*Makes 16 samosas*

1 Place 2¼ cups flour and salt in bowl of electric stand mixer with whisk attachment. Whisk 5 seconds to combine. Add 2 tablespoons oil. Blend until mixture resembles fine bread crumbs. Replace whisk with paddle attachment and add ¾ cup warm water.

2 Mix until dough just comes together, about 45 seconds. Add remaining 3 tablespoons flour. Mix on low speed until smooth and elastic, about 4 minutes. Lightly oil medium bowl; form dough into ball and place in bowl. Cover with towel; set aside 30 to 40 minutes.

3 Cover potatoes with cold water in large pot. Bring to a boil, reduce heat and simmer, covered, until tender, about 20 minutes. Drain and let cool. Peel and dice potatoes into ½-inch pieces.

4 Heat 2 tablespoons oil in large frying pan. Add onions and fry 45 seconds. Add diced potatoes, chilies, if desired, cilantro, cumin seeds, curry and salt. Mix well; cook 1 minute or until curry becomes fragrant. Set aside to cool.

5 Divide dough into 16 equal portions. Roll portions into balls. On floured surface using floured rolling pin, roll 1 ball into 4-inch circle. Place 2 generous teaspoons potato mixture in center of circle.

6 Lift 1 side of dough circle and crease in middle. Lift opposite side of dough and pinch edges of two sides together. Fold up bottom end; pinch closed to form a triangle.

7 Repeat with remaining dough and filling, placing completed Samosas on tray. Refrigerate 1 hour.

8 In heavy, deep skillet over moderate heat, heat 3 to 4 cups oil to 360°F. Working in batches (return oil to 360°F between batches), fry Samosas until golden brown, 1 to 2 minutes per side. Drain on paper towels. Serve warm with Tamarind Sauce.

## Tamarind Sauce

- 2 tablespoons tamarind paste*
- $^1/_3$ cup sugar
- 2 cups water

Place all ingredients in saucepan over medium heat. Bring to a boil and reduce to a low simmer. Simmer until reduced by two-thirds.

*Tamarind paste and tamarind sauce can both be purchased at most well-stocked Indian grocery stores.*

# Mushroom-Onion Tartlets

4 ounces light cream cheese

3 tablespoons butter, divided

3/4 cup plus 1 teaspoon
 all-purpose flour, divided

8 ounces fresh mushrooms,
 coarsely chopped

1/2 cup chopped green onions

1 egg

1/4 cup dried thyme

1/2 cup shredded Swiss cheese

*Makes 24 tartlets*

1 Place cream cheese and 2 tablespoons butter in large bowl of electric stand mixer. Turn mixer to medium-low and beat about 1 minute. Stop and scrape bowl. Add 3/4 cup flour. Reduce speed to low and mix 1 minute or until well blended. Form mixture into ball. Wrap in waxed paper and chill 1 hour. Clean mixer bowl and beater.

2 Divide chilled dough into 24 pieces. Press each piece into miniature muffin cup (greased, if desired).

3 Meanwhile, melt remaining 1 tablespoon butter in 10-inch skillet over medium heat. Add mushrooms and onions. Cook and stir until tender. Remove from heat. Cool slightly.

4 Place egg, remaining 1 teaspoon flour and thyme in mixer bowl. Turn mixer to medium and beat about 30 seconds. Stir in cheese and cooled mushroom mixture. Spoon into pastry-lined muffin cups. Bake at 375°F for 15 to 20 minutes or until egg mixture is puffed and golden brown. Serve warm.

# Appetizer Cream Puffs

1 cup water

¹/₂ cup (1 stick) butter

¹/₄ teaspoon salt

1 cup all-purpose flour

4 eggs

Crab Dill Filling, Chicken and Pineapple Filling, Jerk Shrimp Salad and Creamy Italian Sausage Stuffing (recipes follow)

*Makes 36 cream puffs*

1 Heat water, butter and salt in medium saucepan over high heat to a full rolling boil. Reduce heat and quickly stir in flour, mixing vigorously until mixture leaves sides of pan in ball.

2 Place mixture in bowl of electric stand mixer. Turn to low and add eggs, 1 at a time, mixing about 30 seconds after each addition. Stop and scrape bowl. Turn to medium-low and beat 15 seconds.

3 Drop dough onto greased baking sheets in 36 mounds placed 2 inches apart. Bake at 400°F for 10 minutes. Reduce heat to 350°F and bake 25 minutes longer. Turn off oven. Remove baking sheets from oven. Cut small slit in side of each puff. Return pans to oven for 10 minutes, leaving oven door ajar. Cool completely on wire racks.

4 Cut puffs in half. Pipe or spoon about 1 tablespoon filling into each puff. Serve immediately.

## FILLINGS

### Crab Dill Filling

*Makes 2 cups*

2 cans (6¹/₂ ounces each) crab meat, drained

2 stalks celery, cut into 1-inch pieces

¹/₂ small onion

1 tablespoon lemon juice

¹/₄ teaspoon dill weed

¹/₂ cup mayonnaise

Salt and black pepper

Process crab, celery and onion in food processor. Place crab mixture in bowl of electric stand mixer.

Add lemon juice, dill weed, mayonnaise, salt and pepper. Turn mixer to low and mix 1 minute. Chill mixture thoroughly. Fill cream puffs just before serving as directed above.

### Chicken and Pineapple Filling

*Makes 2 cups*

2 cups cubed cooked chicken

2 stalks celery, cut into 1-inch pieces

1 can (8 ounces) crushed pineapple, drained

¹/₄ cup slivered almonds

¹/₂ cup mayonnaise

¹/₄ teaspoon paprika

Salt and black pepper

Process chicken and celery in food processor. Place chicken mixture in bowl of electric stand mixer.

Add pineapple, almonds, mayonnaise, paprika, salt and pepper. Turn mixer to low and mix 1 minute. Chill mixture thoroughly. Fill cream puffs just before serving as directed above.

## Jerk Shrimp Salad

*Makes 2 cups*

2½  teaspoons Jerk Seasoning (recipe follows)

8  large shrimp, shelled and deveined, tails on

2  tablespoons mayonnaise

½  teaspoon Dijon mustard

2  green onion stalks, trimmed and minced

1  tablespoon finely chopped celery

1  tablespoon finely chopped red bell pepper

Salt and black pepper

Preheat grill or broiler. Brush 2 teaspoons jerk seasoning onto shrimp; place on grill grid or pan sprayed with nonstick cooking spray. Place on grill or under broiler. Cook until pink and just beginning to brown.

Remove shrimp from grill or broiler; allow to cool completely. Remove tails and discard. Slice shrimp in half along back. Chop each half into ¼-inch pieces.

Place shrimp pieces in small bowl. Add remaining jerk seasoning, mayonnaise, mustard, onion, celery and red bell pepper. Add salt and pepper to taste; mix well.

Spoon one generous teaspoon of shrimp salad into each puff.

### Jerk Seasoning

2  tablespoons dark rum

¼  cup water

¼  cup malt vinegar

5  green onions, trimmed and chopped

3  garlic cloves, chopped

2  tablespoons fresh thyme

1  Scotch bonnet chile, stemmed

1  tablespoon vegetable oil

2  teaspoons ground allspice

2  teaspoons ground ginger

2  teaspoons ground cinnamon

1  teaspoon ground nutmeg

1  teaspoon coarse salt

1  teaspoon black pepper

2  teaspoons dark brown sugar

Boil rum and water in small saucepan 1 minute. Transfer rum mixture to food processor; add remaining ingredients. Blend until almost smooth.

## Creamy Italian Sausage Stuffing

*Makes 2 cups*

2  teaspoons olive oil

½  small yellow onion, finely chopped

1  small green Italian frying pepper, stemmed, seeded and chopped

2  (4-inch) sweet Italian sausage links, chopped into ¼-inch pieces

1  clove garlic, mashed

1  tablespoon chopped fresh oregano

¼  cup chicken or vegetable broth

4  tablespoons cream cheese

Salt and black pepper

Heat large skillet over medium heat; add oil. Add onion and frying pepper. Fry until onion is translucent, about 1 minute. Add sausage and toss well, frying until lightly browned, about 2 minutes.

Add garlic and oregano; mix well. Cook 30 seconds. Add broth and cream cheese; mix until cream cheese melts, about 45 seconds. Cook 1 minute more or until sauce is thick and creamy. Add salt and pepper to taste.

Allow to cool slightly, about 5 minutes. Spoon 1 generous teaspoon creamy sausage mixture into each puff.

# Tiropetas

½ pound feta cheese, drained and crumbled

1 package (3 ounces) cream cheese

½ cup cottage cheese

¼ cup grated Romano cheese

⅛ teaspoon black pepper
   Dash ground nutmeg

2 eggs

1 pound frozen prepared phyllo dough, thawed

1 cup (2 sticks) butter, melted

### TIP

*Tiropetas are a traditional Greek layered pastry made with buttered phyllo dough, cheese and spices. Tiropetas are perfect for a savory breakfast or a pre-dinner snack.*

*Makes 4 dozen tiropetas*

1 Place feta cheese, cream cheese and cottage cheese in bowl of electric stand mixer. Turn to medium-low and beat until fluffy, about 1 minute. Stop and scrape bowl. Add Romano cheese, pepper and nutmeg. Turn to low and mix 30 seconds. Stop and scrape bowl. Turn to low and add eggs, 1 at a time, mixing 30 seconds after each addition. Increase speed to medium-low and beat 15 seconds.

2 Place 1 sheet phyllo dough on flat surface. Cover remaining phyllo dough with slightly damp towel. Brush sheet with butter, top with another sheet and brush again with butter. Cut lengthwise into strips, about 2½ inches wide. Place 1 teaspoon cheese mixture on bottom corner of strip. Fold over into triangle shape and continue folding like a flag. Brush with butter and place on greased baking sheet. Repeat with remaining phyllo dough and cheese mixture. Work quickly, as phyllo dough dries out quickly. Bake at 350°F until golden brown, about 15 to 20 minutes. Serve immediately.

# Baba Ghanoush

2 medium eggplants

$1/4$ cup freshly squeezed lemon juice

$1/3$ cup tahini*

3 cloves garlic, minced

$1/4$ teaspoon salt

$1/2$ teaspoon ground cumin

*Tahini is a prepared sesame seed paste used in Mediterranean and Middle Eastern cooking. Look for jars of tahini in the ethnic foods aisle of large supermarkets and in ethnic grocery stores.*

Makes about 2 cups

1 Pierce eggplants all over with a fork. Place on baking sheet and bake at 400°F for 50 to 60 minutes or until eggplants collapse and are soft; cool to room temperature.

2 Slice eggplants from stem to bottom and scrape out flesh with a large spoon. Cut eggplants in half lengthwise and scoop out seed mass; discard seeds. Place remaining flesh in large, fine mesh strainer. Place strainer in bowl or sink and drain well, about 20 minutes.

3 Transfer eggplants to bowl of electric stand mixer; add remaining ingredients. Mix on low until eggplant is beaten smooth and ingredients are well combined. Cover and refrigerate 4 hours or overnight to allow flavors to blend.

# Curry Dip

1 cup mayonnaise

$1/2$ cup sour cream

$1 1/2$ teaspoons lemon juice

1 teaspoon seasoned salt

1 teaspoon chopped fresh parsley

1 teaspoon minced onion

$1/2$ teaspoon Worcestershire sauce

$1/4$ teaspoon salt

$1/4$ teaspoon curry powder

Makes $1 1/2$ cups

Place all ingredients in medium bowl of electric stand mixer. Beat on medium-low 1 minute. Stop and scrape bowl. Beat on high 30 seconds or until creamy. Chill. Serve with raw vegetables.

# Spinach and Cheese Crostini

1 baguette loaf, cut into
  ¹/₂-inch slices
2 teaspoons butter
¹/₂ cup finely chopped onion
1 clove garlic, minced
1 package (9 ounces) frozen
  chopped spinach, thawed
  and squeezed dry
1 package (8 ounces) light
  cream cheese
¹/₄ cup roasted red peppers
¹/₂ cup shredded Cheddar
  cheese

*Makes 24 crostini*

1 Place baguette slices on baking sheet. Bake at 375° F for 4 to 6 minutes or until toasted. Set aside.

2 Melt butter in 10-inch skillet over medium heat. Add onion and garlic. Cook and stir 2 to 3 minutes or until softened. Add spinach. Cook and stir 30 to 60 seconds or until warm. Cool slightly.

3 Place cream cheese in bowl of electric stand mixer. Turn to low; mix about 30 seconds. Add spinach mixture. Continuing on low, mix about 30 seconds more. Spread spinach mixture on toasted baguette slices. Top each slice with about 1 teaspoon Cheddar cheese. Bake at 375°F for 5 to 8 minutes or until thoroughly heated and cheese is melted. Serve warm.

# Cheese Sticks

4 ounces Cheddar cheese
4 ounces Parmesan cheese
¹/₂ teaspoon red pepper flakes
¹/₂ teaspoon dried oregano
1 sheet frozen puff pastry,
  defrosted
1 egg white
1 tablespoon water

TIP

*Always crumble dried herbs between your fingers just before adding to a recipe. This helps release their full flavor.*

*Makes 54 sticks*

1 Shred Cheddar cheese and Parmesan cheese into separate bowls. Add red pepper flakes and oregano to shredded Cheddar cheese and thoroughly combine; set aside.

2 On lightly floured board, roll pastry into 15×18-inch rectangle. Sprinkle Cheddar cheese mixture over pastry and press lightly into dough. Cut pastry lengthwise into 3 (5×18-inch strips) and then horizontally into 1-inch pieces. Twist each piece into a spiral.

3 Beat egg white and water with fork until foamy. Brush sticks with beaten egg white and roll in Parmesan cheese. Place on greased baking sheets and bake at 425°F for 10 to 12 minutes or until golden. Serve warm.

# Tabbouleh in Tomato Cups

4 large firm ripe tomatoes
  (about 8 ounces each)
2 tablespoons olive oil
4 green onions, thinly sliced
1 cup uncooked bulgur wheat
1 cup water
2 tablespoons lemon juice
1 tablespoon chopped fresh
  mint or $\frac{1}{2}$ teaspoon dried
  mint
  Salt and black pepper
  Lemon peel and mint leaves
  (optional)

*Makes 8 servings*

1 Cut tomatoes in half crosswise. Scoop pulp and seeds out of tomatoes into medium bowl, leaving $\frac{1}{4}$-inch-thick shells.

2 Invert tomatoes onto paper towel-lined plate; drain 20 minutes. Chop tomato pulp; set aside.

3 Heat oil in medium saucepan over medium-high heat. Cook and stir green onions 1 to 2 minutes or until wilted. Add bulgur; cook 3 to 5 minutes or until browned.

4 Place vegetable slices in microwaveable bowl with $\frac{1}{4}$ cup water. Cover with plastic wrap and microwave on HIGH 2 minutes. Remove from microwave and set aside to cool. Drain water and pat dry with paper towels.

5 Add reserved tomato pulp, $\frac{3}{4}$ cup water, lemon juice and mint to bulgur mixture. Bring to a boil over high heat; reduce heat to medium-low. Cover; simmer gently 15 to 20 minutes or until liquid is absorbed. Season with salt and pepper. Fill tomato halves with mixture.*

6 Preheat oven to 400°F. Place filled cups in 13×9-inch baking dish; bake 15 minutes or until heated through. Let cool and garnish with lemon peel and mint leaves.

*Tomato cups may be covered and refrigerated at this point up to 24 hours.*

# Sausage Stuffed Mushrooms

30 medium fresh mushrooms

1 slice white bread

1/2 pound pork shoulder, cubed

1 tablespoon chopped fresh parsley

3/4 teaspoon salt

1/4 teaspoon dried sage

1/8 teaspoon black pepper

4 ounces mozzarella cheese, shredded

*Makes 30 mushrooms*

1 Remove stems from mushrooms; set caps aside. Process mushroom stems in food processor; set aside. Place bread in food professor and process into coarse bread crumbs; set aside.

2 Process pork in food processor until ground. Place pork in bowl of electric stand mixer. Add parsley, salt, sage and pepper. Turn mixer to low and mix 1 minute or until well combined. Brown sausage mixture in skillet over medium heat; remove with slotted spoon, leaving fat in pan. Add mushroom stems to fat and cook and stir 3 minutes. Remove from heat and set aside.

3 Combine cheese, mushroom stems, bread crumbs and sausage in large bowl.

4 Fill mushroom caps with sausage/cheese mixture. Place on baking sheets and bake at 450°F for 15 minutes. Serve hot.

# Hummus

1 can (20 ounces) chickpeas, drained

1/4 cup cold water

1/4 cup freshly squeezed lemon juice

1/4 cup tahini (sesame seed paste)

3 cloves garlic, minced

1/2 teaspoon salt

1/4 teaspoon paprika (optional)

*Makes 2 cups*

1 Run chickpeas through food mill and place in bowl of electric stand mixer.

2 Add water, lemon juice, tahini, garlic, salt and paprika, if desired. Turn to medium-low and mix 1 minute. Stop and scrape bowl. Increase speed to high and mix 1 minute more or until smooth.

Crunchy Whole Grain Bread
*(recipe on page 40)*

# breads

Both novices and experts alike will delight in the recipes that follow, which run the gamut from spicy New York Rye to rich, buttery Challah. These simple yet sophisticated recipes make turning out loaves of homemade bread easy and enjoyable. Whether topped with a creamy dollop of butter or a sweet spoonful of preserves, a warm and crusty slice of bread is oh-so satisfying.

# Crunchy Whole Grain Bread

*(photo on page 38)*

1½  cups water

⅓  cup honey

1  tablespoon salt

2  tablespoons vegetable oil

2  packages (4½ teaspoons)
    active dry yeast

½  cup warm water
    (105°F to 115°F)

2  to 2½ cups whole wheat
    flour, divided

1  cup bread flour

1  cup quick or old-fashioned
    oats

½  cup hulled pumpkin seeds
    or sunflower nuts

½  cup assorted grains and
    seeds

1  egg white

1  tablespoon water
    Quick or old-fashioned oats

### TIP

*This bread is a delicious and
healthy way to use leftover grains
and seeds you may have on hand.*

*Makes 2 loaves*

1  Heat water, honey, salt and oil in medium saucepan until warm
(115°F to 120°F).

2  Dissolve yeast in warm water in bowl of electric stand mixer. Let stand
5 minutes. Stir in honey mixture. Add 1 cup whole wheat flour and
bread flour. Mix on low about 2 minutes. Gradually mix or stir in oats,
pumpkin seeds, assorted grains and remaining whole wheat flour, ½ cup
at a time, until dough begins to form ball. Knead 7 to 10 minutes or until
dough is smooth and elastic.

3  Place dough in greased bowl, turning to grease top. Cover; let rise
in warm place 1½ to 2 hours or until doubled in bulk.

4  Grease 2 loaf pans, 9×5-inch or 8½×4½-inch. Punch down dough.
Divide in half. Shape each half into loaf; place in pan. Cover; let rise in
warm place 1 hour or until almost doubled in bulk.

5  Heat oven to 375°F. Combine egg white and water. Brush tops of
loaves with egg mixture. Sprinkle with oats. Bake 35 to 45 minutes or
until loaves sound hollow when tapped. Remove from loaf pans to wire
rack to cool.

# Old-Fashioned Cake Doughnuts

3³/₄ cups all-purpose flour

1 tablespoon baking powder

1 teaspoon ground cinnamon

³/₄ teaspoon salt

¹/₂ teaspoon ground nutmeg

3 eggs

³/₄ cup granulated sugar

1 cup applesauce

2 tablespoons butter, melted

2 cups sifted powdered sugar

3 tablespoons milk

¹/₂ teaspoon vanilla

1 quart vegetable oil

Decorator sprinkles (optional)

*Makes 12 doughnuts and holes*

**1** Combine flour, baking powder, cinnamon, salt and nutmeg in medium bowl. Beat eggs in bowl of electric stand mixer on high until frothy. Gradually beat in granulated sugar on high until thick and pale yellow in color, about 4 minutes. Reduce speed to low; beat in applesauce and butter.

**2** Beat in flour mixture until well blended. Divide dough into halves. Place each half on large piece of plastic wrap. Pat each half into 5-inch square; wrap in plastic wrap. Refrigerate 3 hours or until well chilled.

**3** To prepare glaze, stir together powdered sugar, milk and vanilla in small bowl until smooth. Cover; set aside.

**4** Roll out 1 dough half to ³/₈-inch thickness. Cut dough with floured 3-inch doughnut cutter; repeat with remaining dough. Reserve doughnut holes. Reroll scraps; cut dough again. Heat oil in Dutch oven over medium heat until deep-fry thermometer registers 375°F. Adjust heat as necessary to maintain temperature.

**5** Cook doughnuts and holes in batches for 2 minutes or until golden brown, turning often. Remove with slotted spoon; drain on paper towels. Spread glaze over warm doughnuts; decorate with sprinkles, if desired.

# Classic Deli Pumpernickel Bread

1 cup cold strong coffee*

1/2 cup finely chopped onion

1/2 cup molasses

2 tablespoons butter

1 tablespoon salt

2 packages (4 1/2 teaspoons) active dry yeast

1/2 cup warm water (105°F to 115°F)

2 1/2 cups bread flour, divided

1 cup whole wheat flour

1/4 cup cocoa

1 tablespoon caraway seeds

2 cups medium rye flour

Cornmeal

*Use freshly brewed coffee or instant coffee granules prepared according to package directions.

*Makes 2 loaves*

1 Heat coffee, onion, molasses, butter and salt in medium saucepan until warm (115°F to 120°F).

2 Meanwhile, dissolve yeast in warm water in bowl of electric stand mixer. Let stand 5 minutes. Stir in coffee mixture. Add 2 cups bread flour, whole wheat flour, cocoa and caraway seeds. Mix on low, about 2 minutes. Gradually stir or mix in rye flour, 1/2 cup at a time, and enough remaining bread flour until dough begins to form a ball. Knead 7 to 10 minutes or until dough is smooth and elastic.

3 Place dough in greased bowl, turning to grease top. Cover; let rise in warm place 2 hours or until doubled in bulk.

4 Grease 1 large or 2 small cookie sheets. Sprinkle with cornmeal. Punch down dough. Divide in half. Shape each half into a round, slightly flattened loaf. Place on greased baking sheet(s). Cover; let rise in warm place 1 hour or until almost doubled in bulk.

5 Heat oven to 375°F. Bake 30 to 35 minutes or until loaves sound hollow when tapped. Remove from cookie sheet(s) to wire rack. Brush tops of loaves with butter, if desired.

# New York Rye Bread

2 cups warm water
 (105°F to 115°F)

1/3 cup packed brown sugar

1 tablespoon salt

2 tablespoons vegetable oil

1 package (2 1/4 teaspoons)
 active dry yeast

2 1/2 cups bread flour, divided

1 tablespoon caraway seeds

2 cups rye flour

1 cup whole wheat flour

Shortening

Cornmeal

**TIP**

*New York rye bread is a light rye bread, typically shaped into oblong or round loaves. Try it for delicious deli meat sandwiches or grilled cheese.*

*Makes 2 loaves*

1 Stir together warm water, sugar, salt, oil and yeast in bowl of electric stand mixer until yeast is dissolved.

2 Add 2 cups bread flour. Turn mixer to low and mix about 2 minutes. Gradually mix or stir in caraway seeds, rye and wheat flours, 1/2 cup at a time, and enough remaining bread flour until dough begins to form a ball. Knead 7 to 10 minutes or until dough is smooth and elastic.

3 Place dough in greased bowl, turning to grease top. Cover; let rise in warm place 1 1/2 to 2 hours or until doubled in bulk.

4 Grease 1 large or 2 small cookie sheets with shortening. Sprinkle with cornmeal. Punch down dough. Divide in half. Shape each half into a football-shaped loaf, about 10 inches long. Place loaves on cookie sheet(s). Cover; let rise in warm place 45 to 60 minutes or until almost doubled in bulk.

5 Heat oven to 375°F. Spray or brush loaf with cool water; sprinkle lightly with bread flour. Carefully cut 3 (1/4-inch-deep) slashes on top of loaf with sharp serrated knife.

6 Bake 25 to 30 minutes or until loaves sound hollow when tapped. Remove from cookie sheet(s) to wire rack; cool.

# Crusty Pizza Dough

1 package active dry yeast

1 cup warm water
(105°F to 115°F)

$^1/_2$ teaspoon salt

2 teaspoons olive oil

2$^1/_2$ to 3$^1/_2$ cups all-purpose
flour, divided

1 tablespoon cornmeal

*Makes 4 servings ($^1/_4$ pizza per serving)*

1 Dissolve yeast in warm water in warmed bowl of electric stand mixer with dough hook attachment. Add salt, olive oil and 2$^1/_2$ cups flour. Turn to low and mix about 1 minute.

2 Continuing on low, add remaining flour, $^1/_2$ cup at a time, and mix until dough clings to hook and cleans sides of bowl, about 2 minutes. Knead on low about 2 minutes longer.

3 Place dough in greased bowl, turning to grease top. Cover. Let rise in warm place, free from draft, about 1 hour or until doubled in bulk. Punch dough down.

4 Brush 14-inch pizza pan with oil. Sprinkle with cornmeal. Press dough across bottom of pan, forming a collar around edge to hold toppings. Add toppings as desired. Bake at 450°F for 15 to 20 minutes.

# Basic White Bread

½ cup low-fat (1%) milk

3 tablespoons sugar

2 teaspoons salt

3 tablespoons butter

2 packages active dry yeast

1½ cups warm water (105°F to 115°F)

5 to 6 cups all-purpose flour

*Makes 2 loaves*

1 Place milk, sugar, salt and butter in small saucepan. Heat over low heat until butter melts and sugar dissolves. Cool to lukewarm.

2 Dissolve yeast in warm water in warmed bowl of electric stand mixer with dough hook attachment. Add lukewarm milk mixture and 4½ cups flour. Turn to low and mix about 1 minute.

3 Continuing on low, add remaining flour, ½ cup at a time, and mix until dough clings to hook and cleans sides of bowl, about 2 minutes. Knead on low about 2 minutes longer or until dough is smooth and elastic. Dough will be slightly sticky to the touch.

4 Place dough in greased bowl, turning to grease top. Cover. Let rise in warm place, free from draft, about 1 hour or until doubled in bulk.

5 Punch dough down and divide in half. Shape each half into a loaf, and place in greased 8½×4½×2½-inch loaf pans. Cover. Let rise in warm place, free from draft, about 1 hour or until doubled in bulk.

6 Bake at 400°F until golden brown, about 30 minutes. Remove from pans immediately and cool on wire racks.

Cinnamon Bread: Prepare dough; divide and roll out each half into a rectangle, as directed for Basic White Bread. Mix together ½ cup sugar and 2 teaspoons cinnamon in small bowl. Spread each rectangle with 1 tablespoon softened butter. Sprinkle with half of sugar mixture. Finish rolling and shaping loaves. Place in well-greased 8½×4½×2½-inch loaf pans. Cover. Let rise in warm place, free from draft, about 1 hour or until doubled in bulk. If desired, brush tops with beaten egg white. Bake at 375°F for 40 to 45 minutes or until golden brown. Remove from pans immediately and cool on wire racks.

**Sixty-Minute Rolls:** Increase yeast to 3 packages and sugar to $1/4$ cup. Mix and knead dough as directed for Basic White Bread. Place in greased bowl, turning to grease top. Cover. Let rise in warm place, free from draft, about 15 minutes. Turn dough onto lightly floured surface. Shape as desired (see following suggestions). Cover. Let rise in slightly warm oven (90°F) about 15 minutes. Bake at 425°F for 12 minutes or until golden brown. Remove from pans immediately and cool on wire racks.

**Curlicues:** Divide dough in half and roll each half to 12×9-inch rectangle. Cut 12 equal strips about 1 inch wide. Roll each strip tightly to form a coil, tucking ends underneath. Place on greased baking sheets about 2 inches apart.

**Cloverleafs:** Divide dough into 24 equal pieces. Form each piece into a ball and place in greased muffin pan. With scissors, cut each ball in half, and then into quarters.

# Sour Cream Soda Bread

2 cups all-purpose flour

$3/4$ teaspoon baking soda

$1/2$ teaspoon salt

3 tablespoons sugar

$1/2$ cup (1 stick) butter, softened

$1/2$ cup raisins

1 tablespoon caraway seeds

1 cup sour cream

1 tablespoon milk

*Makes 1 loaf*

1 Place flour, soda, salt, sugar and butter in bowl of electric stand mixer. Turn to medium-low and mix 2 minutes or until mixture is crumbly. Stop and scrape bowl.

2 Add raisins, caraway seeds and sour cream. Reduce speed to low and mix 1 minute or until well blended. Form dough into a mound-shaped circle on greased baking sheet. Brush dough with milk. Bake at 375°F for 45 to 55 minutes. Remove from baking sheet and cool on wire rack.

# Challah

1/3 cup butter, melted

1 cup very warm water (120°F to 130°F)

4 1/2 to 5 1/2 cups all-purpose flour, divided

2 tablespoons sugar

1 1/2 teaspoons salt

1 package active dry yeast

3 eggs

1 egg white

1 egg yolk

1 teaspoon cold water

1 teaspoon poppy seeds

*Makes 2 loaves*

1 Combine butter and water in a bowl or liquid measuring cup; set aside.

2 Place 4 cups flour, sugar, salt and yeast in bowl of electric stand mixer with dough hook attachment. Turn mixer on and mix 1 minute to throughly mix dry ingredients. With mixer running, gradually pour in butter mixture. Mix 1 minute. Add eggs and egg white and mix to incorporate. Mix 1 minute more. Add 1/2 cup flour and mix 1 minute more. Repeat using remaining flour until smooth dough forms. Mix 2 minutes longer.

3 Transfer dough to well-greased bowl, turning to grease top. Cover; let rise in warm place, free from draft, until doubled in bulk, about 1 hour.

4 Punch dough down and divide in half. Divide each half into 3 pieces. Roll each piece into a 14-inch rope. Braid 3 ropes together, tucking ends under, and place on greased baking sheet. Repeat with remaining ropes. Cover; let rise in warm place, free from draft, until doubled in bulk, about 1 hour.

5 Beat egg yolk and water together. Brush loaves with mixture and sprinkle with poppy seeds. Bake at 400°F for 30 to 35 minutes. Remove from baking sheets immediately and cool on wire racks.

# Baking Powder Biscuits

2 cups all-purpose flour

4 teaspoons baking powder

$^1/_2$ teaspoon salt

$^1/_3$ cup shortening

$^2/_3$ cup low-fat (1%) milk

Melted butter (optional)

*Makes 12 biscuits*

1 Place flour, baking powder, salt and shortening in bowl of electric stand mixer. Turn mixer to low and mix about 1 minute. Stop and scrape bowl.

2 Continuing on low, add milk and mix until dough starts to cling to beater. Do not overbeat. Turn dough onto lightly floured surface and knead about 20 seconds or until smooth. Pat or roll to $^1/_2$-inch thickness. Cut with floured 2-inch biscuit cutter.

3 Place on greased baking sheets and brush with melted butter, if desired. Bake at 450°F for 12 to 15 minutes. Serve immediately.

# Russian Black Bread

2 tablespoons vinegar

2 tablespoons dark molasses

1/2 ounce (1/2 square)
  unsweetened chocolate

2 tablespoons butter

1 cup water, divided

1 package active dry yeast

1 cup rye flour*

2 cups all-purpose flour

1/2 cup bran cereal

2 teaspoons caraway seeds

1/2 teaspoon sugar

1 teaspoon salt

1/2 teaspoon instant coffee

1/2 teaspoon onion powder

1/2 teaspoon cornstarch

*You can grind your own rye flour by running
3/4 cup rye berries through a grain mill or
food mill.

*Makes 1 loaf*

1 Heat vinegar, molasses and chocolate in small saucepan over medium heat until chocolate melts. Stir in butter and cool to lukewarm.

2 Heat 3/4 cup water to 105°F to 115°F. Dissolve yeast in warm water.

3 Mix rye flour with all-purpose flour. Place 2 cups flour mixture, cereal, caraway seeds, sugar, salt, coffee and onion powder in bowl of electric stand mixer with dough hook attachment. Turn to low and mix 15 seconds. Continuing on low, gradually add yeast mixture and warm liquids in thin, steady stream, taking about 1 minute. Add remaining flour mixture, 1/2 cup at a time until dough clings to hook** and cleans sides of bowl. Knead on low 2 minutes or until smooth and elastic.

4 Place in greased bowl, turning to grease top. Cover; let rise in warm place, free from draft, until doubled in bulk, about 1 hour.

5 Punch dough down and shape into round loaf. Place in greased 8-inch cake pan. Cover; let rise in warm place, free from draft, until doubled in bulk, about 1 hour.

6 Bake at 350°F for 35 to 40 minutes. Combine remaining 1/4 cup water and cornstarch in small saucepan over medium heat. Stir constantly until mixture comes to a boil; cook 30 seconds. Brush cornstarch mixture over loaf and return to oven for 2 minutes. Remove from pan immediately and cool on wire rack.

**Dough may not form a ball on hook; however, as long as there is contact between dough and hook, kneading will be accomplished. Do not add more than the maximum amount of flour specified or a dry loaf will result.*

# Scones

2 cups all-purpose flour

2 tablespoons sugar

2 teaspoons baking powder

$^1/_2$ teaspoon salt

$^1/_3$ cup butter, softened

2 eggs, divided

$^1/_2$ cup heavy cream

1 teaspoon water

---

**TIP**

*Scones are a classic Scottish quick bread. Originally made of oats and cooked on a griddle, scones are now made of flour and baked. Add flavor to traditional scones with ingredients such as currants, almonds and bits of chocolate.*

*Makes 16 scones*

1 Place flour, sugar, baking powder, salt and butter in bowl of electric stand mixer. Turn to low and mix 30 seconds or until well blended. Stop and scrape bowl.

2 Add 1 egg and cream. Turn to low and mix 30 seconds or until soft dough forms. Knead dough 3 times on lightly floured surface. Divide dough in half. Pat each half into circle about $^1/_2$ inch thick. Cut each circle into 8 wedges.

3 Place wedges 2 inches apart on greased baking sheets. Beat remaining egg and water together. Brush egg mixture over each wedge. Bake at 425°F for 10 to 12 minutes. Serve immediately.

# Orange Muffins

2 cups all-purpose flour

2 teaspoons baking powder

$^1/_2$ teaspoon baking soda

$^1/_4$ teaspoon salt

1 tablespoon grated orange peel

1 egg, beaten

$^3/_4$ cup orange juice

$^1/_4$ cup butter, melted

2 tablespoons milk

1 teaspoon vanilla

Whipped butter (optional)

No-sugar-added orange marmalade fruit spread (optional)

*Makes 12 muffins*

1 Preheat oven to 400°F. Coat 12 medium-size muffin cups with nonstick cooking spray or line with paper baking cups; set aside.

2 Combine flour, baking powder, baking soda, salt and orange peel in medium bowl. Combine egg, orange juice, butter, milk and vanilla in small bowl until blended; stir into flour mixture just until moistened.

3 Spoon batter into prepared muffin cups, filling each cup half full. Bake 18 to 20 minutes or until golden brown. Let cool in pan on wire rack 5 minutes. Remove from pan; cool. Serve warm or at room temperature. Spread with whipped butter and marmalade.

# French Bread

2 packages active dry yeast

2½ cups warm water
(105°F to 115°F)

1 tablespoon salt

1 tablespoon butter, melted

7 cups all-purpose flour

2 tablespoons cornmeal

1 egg white

1 tablespoon cold water

*Makes 2 loaves*

1 Dissolve yeast in warm water in warmed bowl of electric stand mixer with dough hook attachment. Add salt, butter and flour. Turn to low and mix until well blended, about 1 minute. Knead on low about 2 minutes longer. Dough will be sticky.

2 Place dough in greased bowl, turning to grease top. Cover. Let rise in warm place, free from draft, about 1 hour or until doubled in bulk.

3 Punch dough down and divide in half. Roll each half into 12×15-inch rectangle. Roll dough tightly, from longest side, tapering ends if desired. Place loaves on greased baking sheets that have been dusted with cornmeal. Cover. Let rise in warm place, free from draft, about 1 hour or until doubled in bulk.

4 With sharp knife, make 4 diagonal cuts on top of each loaf. Bake at 450°F for 25 minutes. Remove from oven. Beat egg white and water together with a fork. Brush each loaf with egg mixture. Return to oven and bake 5 minutes longer. Remove from baking sheets immediately and cool on wire racks.

# Whole Grain Wheat Bread

1/3 cup plus 1 tablespoon brown
    sugar, divided

2 cups warm water (105°F to
    115°F)

2 packages active dry yeast

5 to 6 cups whole wheat flour

3/4 cup powdered milk

2 teaspoons salt

1/3 cup oil

*Makes 2 loaves*

1 Dissolve 1 tablespoon brown sugar in warm water in small bowl. Add yeast and let mixture stand.

2 Place 4 cups flour, powdered milk, 1/3 cup brown sugar and salt in bowl of electric stand mixer with dough hook attachment. Turn to low and mix about 15 seconds. Continuing on low, gradually add yeast mixture and oil to flour mixture and mix about 1 1/2 minutes longer. Stop and scrape bowl, if necessary.

3 Continuing on low, add remaining flour, 1/2 cup at a time, and mix until dough clings to hook* and cleans sides of bowl, about 2 minutes. Knead on low about 2 minutes longer.

4 Form dough into smooth ball. Place in a greased bowl, turning to grease top. Cover; let rise in warm place, free from draft, until doubled in bulk, about 1 hour.

5 Punch down dough and divide in half. Shape each half into loaf and place in a well-greased 8 1/2×4 1/2-inch loaf pan. Cover; let rise in warm place, free from draft, until doubled in bulk, about 1 hour. Bake at 400°F for 15 minutes. Then reduce heat to 350°F and bake 25 minutes longer. Remove from pans immediately and cool on wire racks.

*Dough may not form a ball on hook. However, as long as hook comes in contact with dough, kneading will be accomplished. Do not add more than the maximum amount of flour specified or a dry loaf will result.*

# Honey Oatmeal **Bread**

1¹/₂  cups water

¹/₂  cup honey

¹/₃  cup butter

5¹/₂ to 6¹/₂ cups all-purpose flour

1  cup quick oats

2  teaspoons salt

2  packages active dry yeast

2  eggs

1  egg white

1  tablespoon water

   Quick oats

*Makes 2 loaves*

1 Place water, honey and butter in small saucepan. Heat over low heat until mixture is very warm (120°F to 130°F).

2 Place 5 cups flour, oats, salt and yeast in bowl of electric stand mixer with dough hook attachment. Turn to low and mix about 15 seconds. Continuing on low, gradually add warm mixture to flour mixture and mix about 1 minute. Add eggs and mix about 1 minute longer.

3 Continuing on low, add remaining flour, ¹/₂ cup at a time, and mix until dough clings to hook and cleans sides of bowl, about 2 minutes. Knead on low about 2 minutes longer.

4 Place dough in greased bowl, turning to grease top. Cover. Let rise in warm place, free from draft, about 1 hour or until doubled in bulk.

5 Punch dough down and divide in half. Shape each half into a loaf. Place in greased 8¹/₂×4¹/₂×2¹/₂-inch loaf pans. Cover. Let rise in warm place, free from draft, about 1 hour or until doubled in bulk.

6 Beat egg white and water together with a fork. Brush tops of loaves with mixture. Sprinkle with oats. Bake at 375°F for 40 minutes. Remove from pans immediately and cool on wire racks.

# Strawberry Muffins

1¹/₄ cups all-purpose flour

2¹/₂ teaspoons baking powder

¹/₂ teaspoon salt

1 cup old-fashioned oats

¹/₂ cup sugar

1 cup milk

¹/₂ cup (1 stick) butter, melted

1 egg, beaten

1 teaspoon vanilla

1 cup chopped fresh
    strawberries

*Makes 12 muffins*

1 Preheat oven to 425°F. Grease bottoms only of 12 standard (2¹/₂-inch) muffin cups or line with paper baking cups; set aside.

2 Combine flour, baking powder and salt in large bowl. Stir in oats and sugar. Combine milk, butter, egg and vanilla in small bowl until well blended; stir into flour mixture just until moistened. Fold in strawberries. Spoon into prepared muffin cups, filling about two-thirds full.

3 Bake 15 to 18 minutes or until lightly browned and toothpick inserted into centers comes out clean. Remove from pan. Cool on wire rack 10 minutes. Serve warm or cool completely.

Eggs Benedict with Smoked Salmon and Hollandaise Sauce *(recipe on page 64)*

# breakfast
## and
# brunch

It is rather simple—and rewarding—to start your day with a gourmet twist. Take a break from the tiresome eggs and toast, and experience just how sublime breakfast and brunch can be.

Sip a spicy Mocha Java Latte alongside crisp Banana-Nut Buttermilk Waffles smothered in sweet maple syrup. These tempting recipes give new meaning to the phrase "rise and shine."

# Eggs Benedict with Smoked Salmon and Hollandaise Sauce

*(photo on page 62)*

4 English muffins, split and toasted

4 ounces sliced smoked salmon

8 tomato slices

Water

1 teaspoon white vinegar

8 eggs

Hollandaise Sauce (recipe follows)

1/3 cup chopped fresh dill

*Makes 4 servings*

1 Preheat oven to 200°F. Place 2 muffin halves, split-side up, on each of 4 serving plates. Divide smoked salmon among muffin halves and place a slice of tomato over salmon. Place plates in oven and turn it off.

2 Fill large skillet with 2 inches water and vinegar; bring to a simmer over medium heat. Break 4 eggs into 4 ramekins (or small bowls). Holding ramekin close to water's surface, slip eggs into water.

3 Cook until whites are completely set and yolks begin to thicken but are not hard, about 3 minutes. Remove eggs with slotted spoon and drain over paper towel. Repeat with remaining eggs; place 1 egg on each prepared muffin half. Spoon a generous tablespoonful of Hollandaise Sauce over each egg and sprinkle with fresh dill.

## Hollandaise Sauce

3 egg yolks

1/4 cup water

2 tablespoons lemon juice

1/2 cup (1 stick) cold butter, cut into 8 pieces

1/4 teaspoon salt (optional)

In small saucepan over low heat, gently whisk egg yolks, water and lemon juice until mixture begins to bubble around edges, about 4 minutes.

Whisk in butter, 1 piece at a time, until butter is melted and sauce has thickened. Whisk in salt, if desired. Do not allow sauce to boil. Serve immediately.

# Apricot Nut Pancakes

2/3 cup whole wheat flour

1/3 cup all-purpose flour

2 teaspoons baking powder

2 tablespoons sugar

1/4 teaspoon salt

3/4 cup milk

2 tablespoons butter, melted

1 egg

1/2 cup dried apricots, finely chopped*

1/2 cup finely chopped walnuts

*Chop apricots by hand or, if desired, place in food processor and pulse until finely chopped.

*Makes 12 pancakes*

1. Combine whole wheat flour, all-purpose flour, baking powder, sugar and salt in medium bowl; set aside.

2. Beat milk, butter and egg in bowl of electric stand mixer on medium-high 30 seconds. With mixer running on low, quickly add flour mixture. Mix 30 seconds. Stop and scrape bowl. Turn mixer to medium-high and beat 30 seconds more or until blended. Reduce speed to low and quickly fold in apricots and walnuts.

3. Slowly heat greased griddle or heavy skillet. Drop 2 tablespoons batter for each pancake at least 1 inch apart on griddle. Cook until bubbles form on surface and edges become dry. Turn and cook until golden brown on other side. Serve immediately.

# Mocha Java Spice Lattes

⅓ cup mini semisweet
   chocolate chips

⅓ cup heavy or whipping
   cream

3 cups strong, freshly brewed
   coffee

1 tablespoon sugar

⅛ teaspoon pumpkin pie spice,
   plus more for garnish

   Whipped cream

*Makes 4 servings*

In medium saucepan over medium heat, whisk chocolate chips, cream, coffee, sugar and pumpkin pie spice until chips are completely melted and mixture just starts to boil. Divide among 4 tall Irish coffee (or regular coffee) mugs. Top each with whipped cream and a sprinkling of pumpkin pie spice.

# Whole Wheat Pancakes

¾ cup milk

2 tablespoons butter, melted

1 egg

⅓ cup whole wheat flour

⅔ cup all-purpose flour

2 teaspoons baking powder

2 tablespoons sugar

¼ teaspoon salt

*Makes 10 pancakes*

1 Place milk, butter and egg in bowl of electric stand mixer. Turn mixer to medium-low and whip 30 seconds. Add whole wheat flour, all-purpose flour, baking powder, sugar and salt. Increase speed to medium and whip until combined, about 30 seconds.

2 Slowly heat greased griddle or heavy skillet. Using 2 tablespoons batter for each pancake, drop onto griddle. Cook until bubbles form on surface and edges become dry. Turn and cook until golden brown on underside. Serve immediately.

Mocha Java Spice Lattes

# Chicken Chilaquiles with Salsa Chipotle

Salsa Chipotle (recipe
follows)

12 (6- or 7-inch) corn tortillas

1½ to 2½ tablespoons vegetable
oil, divided

2 cups shredded cooked
chicken

6 eggs, beaten

1 cup shredded queso
Chihuahua or manchego
cheese

½ cup finely crumbled queso
añejo or feta cheese

⅓ cup crema Mexicana* or
crème fraîche

*Crema Mexicana is a dairy product similar
to sour cream or crème fraîche, either of
which can be substituted if you are unable to
find crema in your supermarket's dairy case.
Crema Mexicana is sweeter and creamier
than crème fraîche, but it has a slightly
bolder flavor than sour cream.

*Makes 6 to 8 servings*

1 Prepare Salsa Chipotle; set aside. Preheat oven to 375°F. Spray
13×9-inch baking dish with nonstick cooking spray.

2 Arrange all tortillas in single stack on cutting board. Slice into
¼- to ½-inch-wide ribbons with sharp knife. Heat 1½ tablespoons
vegetable oil in large skillet over medium-high heat until shimmering. Add
half the tortilla strips and fry until golden brown, gently stirring often to
prevent tortilla strips from sticking to one another. Transfer with slotted
spoon to prepared baking dish. Add remaining oil to skillet, if needed, and
repeat with remaining tortilla strips.

3 Add chicken to baking dish. Pour Salsa Chipotle over tortilla strips
and chicken and toss gently to coat evenly. Stir in beaten eggs.
Cover with foil and bake 35 minutes or until tortilla strips have absorbed
enough sauce to become soft but not soggy and casserole is heated
through. Remove from oven; remove foil and sprinkle with queso
Chihuahua. Return to oven and bake 5 to 10 minutes or until cheese has
melted and casserole is beginning to brown on top and edges.

4 Remove from oven and cool slightly before serving. Sprinkle each
serving with crumbled queso añejo and drizzle with crema Mexicana
or garnish as desired.

## Salsa Chipotle

1 to 1½ pounds fresh ripe tomatoes*

2 tablespoons vegetable oil, divided

2 to 3 canned chipotle peppers in adobo sauce

½ large white onion, sliced ¼ inch thick

3 cloves garlic, finely chopped

2½ cups chicken or vegetable broth, plus extra if needed

½ cup finely chopped fresh cilantro

Salt

*Or substitute 1 can (28 ounces) whole tomatoes, drained. Do not broil as directed below but proceed to blending step.*

Preheat broiler. Place tomatoes in large bowl. Pour 1 tablespoon oil over tomatoes and gently roll to coat. Place tomatoes on broiling pan. Broil, 4 inches from heat, about 6 minutes or until darkly roasted (evenly blackened in spots). Turn tomatoes over and roast other side. Remove from broiler and let cool. Working over broiler pan, remove and discard tomato peels. Remove and discard tomato cores if still hard.

Transfer tomatoes to blender along with any juice collected in broiler pan. Add chipotle peppers. Blend using on/off pulses until ground to a thick, coarse purée.

Heat remaining oil in Dutch oven over medium heat. Add onion and cook, stirring frequently, until golden brown. Add garlic and cook 1 minute. Pour in purée from blender and cook until mixture comes to a boil and thickens, about 5 minutes. Stir in broth. Remove from heat and allow mixture to cool to room temperature. Stir in additional broth, if necessary, to bring mixture to 4½ cups total. Stir in cilantro and season to taste with salt. Salsa can be prepared up to 4 days in advance and refrigerated in an airtight container until needed.

# Banana-Nut Buttermilk Waffles

³/₄ cup walnuts or pecans

2 cups all-purpose flour

¹/₄ cup sugar

2 teaspoons baking powder

1 teaspoon salt

2 eggs, separated

2 cups buttermilk

2 very ripe bananas, mashed
(about 1 cup)

4 tablespoons butter, melted

1 teaspoon vanilla

Syrup

Banana slices

Additional walnuts
(optional)

*Makes 4 servings*

1 Toast walnuts in medium nonstick skillet over medium heat 5 to 8 minutes until fragrant, stirring frequently. Transfer to plate to cool; chop and set aside.

2 Lightly spray waffle iron with nonstick cooking spray; preheat according to manufacturer's directions.

3 Meanwhile, combine flour, sugar, baking powder and salt in large bowl. Beat egg yolks in medium bowl. Add buttermilk, mashed bananas, butter, vanilla and walnuts; mix well. Stir buttermilk mixture into flour mixture just until moistened.

4 Beat egg whites in bowl of electric stand mixer on high until stiff but not dry. Fold egg whites into batter.

5 Pour ³/₄ cup batter into waffle iron; bake 4 to 6 minutes or until golden. Serve with syrup and banana slices. Garnish with additional walnuts.

# Chunky Fruity Homemade Granola

2 cups organic old-fashioned oats

1⅓ cups raw, slivered almonds

1 cup sweetened flaked coconut

3 tablespoons unsalted butter

¼ cup organic honey

1 cup (⅜-inch dice) dried apricots

¾ cup dried cranberries

¾ cup dried tart cherries

½ cup dried blueberries

½ cup roasted, unsalted cashew pieces

**TIP**

*Granola is a great grab-and-go snack! Add it to a cup of yogurt, or sprinkle over ice cream.*

*Makes 2 (1-quart) jars*

1 Preheat oven to 300°F. Line baking sheet with foil or parchment paper. Set aside.

2 Combine oats, almonds and coconut in large mixing bowl. Melt butter in microwave in microwaveable glass measuring cup on HIGH 30 to 50 seconds (time will vary depending on power of your microwave). Add honey. Whisk mixture to blend. Pour butter mixture over oat mixture and toss with rubber spatula to evenly coat. Transfer mixture to prepared baking sheet, spreading evenly. Bake 20 to 25 minutes or until golden, stirring once or twice. Remove pan from oven and cool completely on wire rack.

3 Combine remaining ingredients in large mixing bowl. Crumble cooled oat mixture and add to fruit mixture. Stir together to combine. Transfer granola to 2 (1-quart) wide-mouth jars. Seal jars.

# Quick Breakfast Empanadas

½ pound bacon (about 10 slices)

1 package (15 ounces) refrigerated pie crust

9 eggs, divided

1 teaspoon water

1 teaspoon salt

Dash black pepper

1 tablespoon butter

2 cups (8 ounces) Mexican-style shredded cheese, divided

4 tablespoons salsa

*Makes 4 servings*

1 Preheat oven to 425°F. Spray baking sheet with nonstick cooking spray. Cook bacon in large skillet over medium-high heat until crisp; drain on paper towels and wipe out skillet. Chop bacon into ¼-inch pieces. Cut pie crusts in half to make 4 semicircles; place on prepared baking sheet.

2 Beat 1 egg and water in small bowl until well blended; set aside. Beat remaining 8 eggs, salt and pepper in medium bowl until well blended. Heat large skillet over medium heat. Add butter; tilt skillet to coat bottom. Sprinkle bacon evenly in skillet. Pour eggs into skillet and cook 2 minutes without stirring; gently stir until eggs form large curds and are still slightly moist. Transfer to plate to cool.

3 Spoon one-fourth of cooled scrambled egg mixture onto half of each semicircle of pie crust. Reserve ¼ cup cheese; sprinkle remaining cheese evenly over eggs. Top with salsa.

4 Brush inside edges of each semicircle with reserved egg-water mixture. Fold dough over top of egg mixture and seal edges with fork, making 4 empanadas. (Flour fork tines to prevent sticking, if necessary.)

5 Brush tops of empanadas with remaining egg-water mixture and sprinkle with reserved cheese. Bake 15 to 20 minutes or until golden.

# Oatmeal Brulée with Raspberry Sauce

## Brulée

- 4 cups water
- 1/2 teaspoon salt
- 3 cups old-fashioned oats
- 1 cup whipping cream
- 1/2 teaspoon vanilla
- 1/4 cup granulated sugar
- 3 egg yolks
- 3 tablespoons brown sugar

## Raspberry Sauce

- 6 ounces frozen sweetened raspberries
- 1/2 cup granulated sugar
- 1/4 cup water
- 1 teaspoon orange extract

### NOTE

*This brulée has the texture of rice pudding and the taste of sweet custard, with a crème brulée-like topping. **Brulée** (broo-LAY) comes from the French word for "burned."*

*Makes 4 servings*

1. For Brulée: Preheat oven to 300°F. Line baking sheet with foil; set aside. In medium saucepan, heat 4 cups water and salt over high heat. When water simmers, add oats and reduce heat to low. Cook, stirring occasionally, 3 to 5 minutes, or until water is absorbed and oats are tender. Divide oatmeal among 4 large ramekins or ovenproof bowls. Place on prepared baking sheet; set aside.

2. In separate medium saucepan, scald cream over high heat; do not boil. Remove from heat; stir in vanilla. In small bowl, mix granulated sugar and egg yolks with fork or whisk. Pour about 1/2 cup scalded cream in a thin stream into egg mixture, stirring quickly; stir egg mixture into saucepan of scalded cream, whisking until well blended and smooth. Ladle cream mixture equally over oatmeal in ramekins. Bake 35 minutes or until nearly set. Remove from oven; preheat broiler to 500°F.

3. For Raspberry Sauce: While brulées are baking, purée raspberries, granulated sugar, water and orange extract in blender or food processor. Pour sauce through strainer to remove seeds; discard seeds.

4. Sprinkle 1 1/2 teaspoons brown sugar evenly over each brulée. Place baking sheet under broiler; broil 3 to 5 minutes or until tops are caramelized. Cool 5 to 10 minutes before serving. Serve with Raspberry Sauce.

# Bacon and Egg Cups

12 slices bacon, cut into thirds

6 eggs or 1½ cups egg
  substitute

½ cup half-and-half

½ cup diced bell peppers (red,
  green or a combination)

½ cup shredded Monterey
  Jack cheese with jalapeño
  peppers

¼ teaspoon salt

¼ teaspoon black pepper

**TIP**

*To save prep time, look for mixed
diced bell peppers in the produce
section of the grocery store.*

*Makes 12 servings*

1 Preheat oven to 350°F. Lightly spray 12-cup standard (2½-inch)
  muffin pan with nonstick cooking spray.

2 Arrange bacon slices flat in single layer on plate lined with paper
  towel. Do not overlap. Top with additional sheets of paper towel and
microwave on HIGH 2 to 3 minutes or until cooked yet pliable. Place
3 bacon slices in each cup, overlapping 1 inch in bottom of cup.

3 Beat eggs, half-and-half, bell peppers, cheese, salt and pepper in
  medium bowl until well blended. Fill each cup with ¼ cup egg
mixture. Bake 20 to 25 minutes or until eggs are set in center. Run knife
around edge of each cup before removing from pan.

# Apple Crumb Coffee Cake

1/2 cup milk

1/4 cup (1/2 stick) butter

1/4 cup warm water
   (105°F to 115°F)

3 to 3 1/2 cups all–purpose
   flour, divided

1/4 cup sugar

1 teaspoon salt

1 package active dry yeast

1 egg

Cinnamon Crumb Filling
   (recipe follows)

2 apples, peeled, cored and
   thinly sliced

*Makes 1 coffee cake*

1 Scald milk; add butter and water. Cool to lukewarm. Place 2 cups flour, sugar, salt and yeast in bowl of electric stand mixer with dough hook attachment. Turn to low and mix 15 seconds. Gradually add warm liquid to bowl, mixing 1 minute. Add egg and mix 1 minute longer. Continuing on low, add remaining flour, 1/2 cup at a time, until dough clings to hook and cleans sides of bowl. Knead on low 2 minutes longer.

2 Place in greased bowl, turning to grease top. Cover; let rise in warm place, free from draft, until doubled in bulk, about 1 hour.

3 Punch down dough and divide in half. Roll each half to 9-inch circle. Place 1 circle in bottom of greased 9-inch springform pan. Sprinkle one-fourth of Cinnamon Crumb Filling over dough. Arrange half the apple slices on filling; sprinkle another one-fourth filling over apples. Place remaining dough circle in pan and repeat layers with remaining crumb mixture and apples. Cover; let rise in warm place, free from draft, until doubled in bulk, about 1 hour.

4 Bake at 375°F for 45 to 50 minutes. Remove sides of springform pan immediately and cool on wire rack.

## Cinnamon Crumb Filling

1 cup sugar

3/4 cup all–purpose flour

2 1/2 teaspoons ground cinnamon

6 tablespoons butter

Mix all ingredients with fork until crumbly.

# Crispy Waffles

2 cups all-purpose flour
3 teaspoons baking powder
2 tablespoons sugar
1/2 teaspoon salt
2 eggs, separated
1 1/4 cups low-fat (1%) milk
1/4 cup butter, melted

*Makes 6 waffles*

1 Combine flour, baking powder, sugar and salt in bowl of electric stand mixer. Add egg yolks, milk and butter. Turn mixer to medium-low and mix until ingredients are combined, about 30 seconds. Stop and scrape bowl. Continuing on medium-low, mix until smooth, about 15 seconds. Pour mixture into another bowl. Clean mixer bowl.

2 Place egg whites in mixer bowl. Turn speed to medium-high and whip until egg whites are stiff but not dry. Gently fold egg whites into flour mixture.

3 Spray waffle iron with nonstick cooking spray. Heat waffle iron according to manufacturer's directions. Pour about 1/3 cup batter for each waffle onto iron. Bake 3 to 5 minutes or until golden brown.

# Pancakes

1 1/2 cups all-purpose flour
2 teaspoons baking powder
1 teaspoon sugar
1/2 teaspoon salt
1/2 cup egg substitute or 2 eggs
1 1/4 cups low-fat (1%) milk
3 tablespoons shortening, melted

*Makes 8 pancakes*

1 Combine flour, baking powder, sugar and salt in bowl of electric stand mixer. Add remaining ingredients. Turn to medium-low and mix until ingredients are combined, about 30 seconds. Stop and scrape bowl. Turn speed to medium-low and mix until smooth, about 15 seconds.

2 Spray griddle or heavy skillet with nonstick cooking spray. Heat griddle to medium-high heat. Pour about 1/3 cup batter for each pancake onto griddle. Cook 1 to 2 minutes or until bubbles form on surface and edges become dry. Turn and cook 1 to 2 minutes longer or until golden brown on underside.

# Blueberry Macadamia Nut Swirl Coffee Cake

1¾ cups all-purpose flour

½ cup whole wheat flour

¾ cup firmly packed brown sugar

¾ cup (1½ sticks) butter, chilled and cut into small pieces

1 teaspoon baking powder

½ teaspoon baking soda

¼ teaspoon salt

¾ cup buttermilk

1 egg

1 cup blueberry pie filling

¾ cup chopped macadamia nuts or blanched almonds

*Makes 1 cake*

1 Place all-purpose flour, whole wheat flour, brown sugar and butter in bowl of electric stand mixer. Turn mixer to low and mix until butter is the size of peas, about 3 minutes. Stop and scrape bowl. Remove ½ cup flour mixture. Set aside.

2 Add baking powder, baking soda and salt to flour mixture. Turn mixer to low and mix 30 seconds. Add buttermilk and egg. Continuing on low, mix just until moistened, about 30 seconds. Do not overbeat.

3 Spoon batter into greased 13×9×2-inch baking pan. Drop blueberry filling by tablespoonfuls on top of batter; swirl into batter. Sprinkle top with nuts and reserved flour mixture. Bake at 350°F for 30 to 40 minutes or until light golden brown.

# Apple Cinnamon French Toast Casserole

1 large loaf French bread, cut into 1½-inch-thick slices
3½ cups milk
9 eggs
1½ cups sugar, divided
1 tablespoon vanilla
½ teaspoon salt
6 to 8 medium baking apples, such as McIntosh or Cortland, peeled and sliced
1 teaspoon ground cinnamon
½ teaspoon ground nutmeg

*Makes 6 to 8 servings*

1 Place bread slices in greased 13×9-inch glass baking dish or casserole dish.

2 Whisk milk, eggs, 1 cup sugar, vanilla and salt in large bowl until well blended. Pour half of mixture over bread.

3 Layer apple slices over bread. Pour remaining half of egg mixture over apples.

4 Combine remaining ½ cup sugar, cinnamon and nutmeg in small bowl; sprinkle over casserole. Cover and refrigerate overnight.

5 Preheat oven to 350°F. Bake, uncovered, 1 hour or until eggs are set.

# Peach Pecan Upside-Down Pancake

2 tablespoons butter, melted

2 tablespoons packed light brown sugar

1 tablespoon maple syrup

½ package (1 pound) frozen unsweetened peach slices, thawed

2 to 3 tablespoons pecan pieces

2 eggs

⅓ cup milk

½ teaspoon vanilla

⅔ cup biscuit baking mix

Additional maple syrup (optional)

*Makes 6 servings*

1 Preheat oven to 400°F. Spray 8- or 9-inch pie pan with nonstick cooking spray.

2 Pour butter into pie pan. Sprinkle on brown sugar and maple syrup. Place peach slices in single layer on top in a decorative circle. Sprinkle with pecans; set aside.

3 Whisk together eggs, milk and vanilla in medium bowl. Stir in baking mix until just combined. Pour batter over peaches. Bake 15 to 18 minutes until lightly browned and firm to the touch. Remove from oven. Let cool 1 minute. Run knife around outer edge. Invert pancake onto serving plate. Serve immediately with additional maple syrup.

Carrot Cake *(recipe on page 86)*

# cakes

If "let them eat cake" is your mantra, then this collection of cake and frosting recipes just might change your life.

Master the time-tested classics such as Carrot Cake with rich Cream Cheese Frosting, or experiment with enticing new ideas such as Cappuccino Fudge Cupcakes. Your sugary creations will make every day feel like a celebration.

# Carrot Cake

*(photo on page 84)*

6 eggs

1 1/2 cups (3 sticks) butter, melted

3 cups all-purpose flour

2 cups sugar

2 teaspoons baking powder

1/2 teaspoon salt

1 1/2 teaspoons ground cinnamon

3 cups finely grated carrots

3/4 cup chopped walnuts

Cream Cheese Frosting
(recipe follows)

*Makes 1 cake*

1 Place eggs and butter in bowl of electric stand mixer. Turn to medium and beat 1 minute. Stop and scrape bowl. Add flour, sugar, baking powder, salt and cinnamon. Reduce speed to low and beat 30 seconds or just until combined. Continue mixing on low and quickly fold in carrots and walnuts, about 10 seconds.

2 Split batter between 2 greased and floured 8-inch springform pans. Bake at 350°F for 55 to 60 minutes. Cakes are very moist and should not be tested for doneness with inserted toothpick. Remove cakes from oven at end of baking period. Cool in pans 10 minutes, and then remove and cool on wire rack. Frost layers with Cream Cheese Frosting.

## Cream Cheese Frosting

*Makes 3 cups*

4 packages (3 ounces each) cream cheese, softened

1/2 cup (1 stick) butter, softened

2 teaspoons vanilla

2 1/2 cups powdered sugar

1 Place cream cheese, butter and vanilla in bowl of electric stand mixer. Turn to medium and beat 2 minutes. Stop and scrape bowl.

2 Sift powdered sugar into bowl. Turn to low and mix 30 seconds or just until combined. Stop and scrape bowl. Turn to medium and beat 2 minutes. Refrigerate until ready to use.

# Caramel Crème Frosting

1/2 cup (1 stick) butter

1 cup packed brown sugar

1/4 cup low-fat (1%) milk

1 cup miniature marshmallows

2 cups powdered sugar

1/2 teaspoon vanilla

*Frosting for 2-layer or 13×9×2-inch cake*

1 Melt butter in medium saucepan. Add brown sugar and milk, stirring to blend. Heat to boiling. Cook about 1 minute, stirring constantly. Remove from heat. Add marshmallows. Stir until marshmallows melt and mixture is smooth.

2 Place powdered sugar in bowl of electric stand mixer. Add brown sugar mixture and vanilla. Turn to low and mix about 30 seconds. Turn to medium and beat about 1 minute or until smooth and creamy. Spread on cake while warm; frosting sets as it cools.

# Classic Chocolate Cake

2 cups all-purpose flour

1 1/3 cups sugar

1 teaspoon baking powder

1/2 teaspoon baking soda

1/2 teaspoon salt

1/2 cup shortening

1 cup low-fat (1%) milk

1 teaspoon vanilla

2 eggs

2 squares (1 ounce each) unsweetened chocolate, melted

*Makes 1 cake*

1 Combine dry ingredients in bowl of electric stand mixer. Add shortening, milk and vanilla. Turn mixer to low and mix about 1 minute. Stop and scrape bowl. Add eggs and chocolate. Continuing on low, mix about 30 seconds. Stop and scrape bowl. Turn to medium and beat about 1 minute.

2 Pour batter into 2 greased and floured 8- or 9-inch round baking pans. Bake at 350°F for 30 to 35 minutes or until toothpick inserted into center comes out clean. Cool 10 minutes. Remove from pans. Cool completely on wire rack. Frost, if desired.

# German Chocolate Cake

¹/₂ cup hot water

4 squares (1 ounce each)
   semisweet chocolate

1 cup (2 sticks) butter,
   softened

2 cups sugar

4 eggs

2¹/₄ cups all-purpose flour

1 teaspoon baking soda

¹/₂ teaspoon salt

1 cup buttermilk

1 teaspoon vanilla

   Coconut Pecan Frosting
   (recipe follows)

*Makes 1 cake*

1 Place water and chocolate in double boiler. Stir chocolate constantly over boiling water until it melts; set aside.

2 Beat butter and sugar in bowl of electric stand mixer about 2 minutes or until fluffy. Stop and scrape bowl. Turn to medium and add eggs, 1 at a time, beating 15 seconds after each addition. Continuing on medium, add chocolate mixture and beat 15 seconds more or just until incorporated. Stop and scrape bowl.

3 Add flour, soda, salt, buttermilk and vanilla. Turn to low and mix until well blended, about 30 seconds.

4 Divide batter evenly between 2 greased and floured 9-inch cake pans. Bake at 350°F for 35 to 45 minutes. Cool in pans 10 minutes, and then remove and cool completely on wire racks. Frost middle layer and top with Coconut Pecan Frosting.

## Coconut Pecan Frosting

*Makes 3 cups*

1 cup sugar

³/₄ cup evaporated milk

3 eggs, beaten

¹/₃ cup butter

1 cup sweetened flaked coconut

1 cup chopped pecans

1 Combine sugar, evaporated milk, eggs and butter in large saucepan. Cook and stir over medium heat until mixture begins to thicken.

2 Remove from heat and place in bowl of electric stand mixer. Add coconut and pecans. Mix on low until thick and spreadable. Refrigerate until ready to use.

# Marble Cheesecake

1 cup graham cracker crumbs

1/4 cup packed brown sugar

3 tablespoons butter, melted

4 packages (8 ounces each)
  cream cheese, softened

2 teaspoons vanilla

1 3/4 cups granulated sugar

4 eggs

2 squares (1 ounce each)
  unsweetened chocolate,
  melted

*Makes 1 cheesecake*

1 Stir together graham cracker crumbs, brown sugar and butter. Press mixture into bottom of 9-inch springform pan.

2 Beat cream cheese, vanilla and sugar in bowl of electric stand mixer on medium-high 2 minutes or until fluffy. Stop and scrape bowl. Turn to low and add eggs, 1 at a time, mixing 15 seconds after each addition. Stop and scrape bowl. Turn to medium and beat 30 seconds.

3 Pour one-third of cream cheese mixture into small bowl. Add chocolate and mix well. Drop chocolate and plain batter by the spoonful into prepared pan. Swirl lightly with knife. Bake at 325°F for 1 hour 30 minutes. Cool on wire rack 30 minutes, and then refrigerate at least 2 hours.

# Angel Food Cake

1¼ cups all-purpose flour

1½ cups sugar, divided

1½ cups egg whites (about
12 to 15 egg whites)

1½ teaspoons cream of tartar

¼ teaspoon salt

1½ teaspoons vanilla or
½ teaspoon almond extract

*Makes 16 servings*

1 Mix flour and ½ cup sugar in small bowl. Set aside. Place egg whites in bowl of electric stand mixer. Gradually turn speed to medium and whip until egg whites are frothy, 30 to 60 seconds.

2 Add cream of tartar, salt and vanilla. Turn to medium-high and whip until whites are almost stiff but not dry, 2 to 2½ minutes. Reduce speed to low. Gradually add remaining 1 cup sugar and mix about 1 minute. Stop and scrape bowl. Remove bowl from mixer. Spoon flour-sugar mixture, ¼ cup at a time, over egg whites. Fold in gently with spatula just until blended.

3 Pour batter into ungreased 10-inch tube pan. With knife, gently cut through batter to break up large air bubbles. Bake at 375°F until crust is golden brown and cracks are very dry, about 35 minutes. Immediately invert cake pan onto funnel or soft drink bottle. Cool completely. Remove from pan.

# Quick Yellow Cake

2¼ cups all-purpose flour

1⅓ cups sugar

3 teaspoons baking powder

½ teaspoon salt

½ cup shortening

1 cup low-fat (1%) milk

1 teaspoon vanilla

2 eggs

*Makes 1 cake*

1 Combine dry ingredients in bowl of electric stand mixer. Add shortening, milk and vanilla. Turn to low and mix about 1 minute. Stop and scrape bowl. Add eggs. Continuing on low, mix about 30 seconds. Stop and scrape bowl. Increase speed to medium and beat about 1 minute.

2 Pour batter into 2 greased and floured 8- or 9-inch round baking pans. Bake at 350°F for 30 to 35 minutes or until toothpick inserted into center comes out clean. Cool 10 minutes. Remove from pans. Cool completely on wire rack. Frost, if desired.

# Cappuccino Fudge Cupcakes

½ cup (1 stick) butter, softened

1½ cups sugar

3 eggs

1 tablespoon plus 2 teaspoons instant espresso or coffee granules

¾ cup milk

1¾ cups all-purpose flour

1½ teaspoons baking powder

¼ teaspoon salt

Coffee Cream (recipe follows)

Fudge Sauce (recipe follows)

*Makes 8 cupcakes*

1 Beat butter in bowl of electric stand mixer on medium-high until creamy. Add sugar gradually with mixer running and beat 3 minutes or until light and fluffy. Reduce speed to medium and add eggs, 1 at a time, beating 30 seconds after each addition. Stop and scrape bowl. Dissolve instant espresso in milk. Set aside.

2 Combine flour, baking powder and salt. Turn mixer to low and add a third of flour mixture alternately with half of milk mixture, mixing 15 seconds after each addition.

3 Spoon batter into 8 greased and floured custard cups. Place cups on baking sheet. Bake at 350°F for 30 to 35 minutes or until toothpick inserted into cupcake comes out clean. Remove from custard cups and cool on wire rack. Top with Coffee Cream and serve with Fudge Sauce.

## Coffee Cream

*Makes about 2½ cups*

1½ cups heavy cream

¼ cup sugar

1½ teaspoons instant espresso or coffee granules

Beat cream, sugar and instant espresso in bowl of electric stand mixer on high until stiff.

## Fudge Sauce

4 squares (1 ounce each) semisweet chocolate

½ cup whipping cream

½ teaspoon ground cinnamon

Place chocolate, cream and cinnamon in small saucepan. Cook and stir over low heat until chocolate is melted and mixture is combined.

# Pumpkin Cheesecake with Gingersnap-Pecan Crust

## Crust

1¼ cups gingersnap cookie crumbs (about 24 cookies)

⅓ cup pecans, very finely chopped

¼ cup granulated sugar

¼ cup (½ stick) butter, melted

## Filling

3 packages (8 ounces each) cream cheese, softened

1 cup packed light brown sugar

1 teaspoon ground cinnamon

½ teaspoon ground ginger

¼ teaspoon ground nutmeg

2 eggs

2 egg yolks

1 cup solid-pack pumpkin

**TIP**

*To help prevent the cheesecake from cracking while baking, place a pan of water in the oven to create moist heat.*

*Makes 10 to 12 servings*

1 Preheat oven to 350°F. For crust, combine cookie crumbs, pecans, sugar and butter in medium bowl; mix well. Press crumb mixture evenly into bottom of ungreased 9-inch springform pan. Bake 8 to 10 minutes or until golden brown.

2 Meanwhile, for filling, beat cream cheese in bowl of electric stand mixer at medium until fluffy. Add brown sugar, cinnamon, ginger and nutmeg; beat until well blended. Beat in eggs and egg yolks, 1 at a time, beating well after each addition. Beat in pumpkin.

3 Pour mixture into baked crust. Bake 1 hour or until edges are set but center is still moist. Turn off oven; let cheesecake stand in oven with door ajar 30 minutes. Transfer to wire rack. To prevent cracking, loosen edges of cake from rim of pan with thin metal spatula; cool completely. Cover; refrigerate at least 24 hours or up to 48 hours before serving.

# Easy White Cake

2 cups all-purpose flour
1½ cups sugar
3 teaspoons baking powder
½ teaspoon salt
½ cup shortening
1 cup low-fat (1%) milk
1 teaspoon vanilla
4 egg whites

*Makes 1 cake*

1 Combine dry ingredients in bowl of electric stand mixer. Add shortening, milk and vanilla. Turn speed to low and mix about 1 minute. Stop and scrape bowl. Add egg whites. Turn speed to medium and beat about 1 minute or until smooth and fluffy.

2 Pour batter into 2 greased and floured 8- or 9-inch round baking pans. Bake at 350°F for 30 to 35 minutes or until toothpick inserted into center comes out clean. Cool 10 minutes. Remove from pans. Cool completely on wire rack. Frost, if desired.

# Buttercream Frosting

¾ cup (1½ sticks) butter, softened
2 cups powdered sugar
1½ teaspoons vanilla

*Makes frosting for 2-layer or 13×9×2-inch cake*

1 Place butter in bowl of electric stand mixer. Turn to medium and beat 30 seconds. Stop and scrape bowl.

2 Sift powdered sugar into bowl. Add vanilla. Reduce speed to low and beat 30 seconds. Stop and scrape bowl. Turn speed to medium and beat 2 minutes or until fluffy.

# Chocolate Frosting

1 cup (2 sticks) butter,
  softened

2 tablespoons light corn syrup

4 cups powdered sugar

2 squares (1 ounce each)
  unsweetened chocolate,
  melted

*Makes frosting for 2-layer or 13×9×2-inch cake*

1 Place butter in bowl of electric stand mixer. Turn mixer to medium-low and beat 1½ minutes or until creamy. Stop and scrape bowl. Add corn syrup. Reduce speed to low and mix well. Stop and scrape bowl.

2 Continue mixing on low. Gradually add powdered sugar, mixing until blended. Turn speed to medium-low and beat about 1 minute. Stop and scrape bowl. Reduce speed to low. Slowly add melted chocolate and mix about 1½ minutes. Stop and scrape bowl. Turn speed to medium-low and beat about 1 minute.

# Sour Cream Bundt Cake

3 cups all-purpose flour

$1/2$ teaspoon salt

3 teaspoons baking powder

1 teaspoon baking soda

$1^1/_2$ cups sugar

1 teaspoon ground cinnamon

1 cup (2 sticks) butter, softened

1 cup sour cream

1 teaspoon vanilla

3 eggs

1 cup chopped nuts

*Makes 1 cake*

1 Sift flour, salt, baking powder, baking soda, sugar and cinnamon into bowl of electric stand mixer. Add butter, sour cream and vanilla. Turn mixer to low and mix until ingredients are combined, about 30 seconds. Stop and scrape bowl. Turn to medium-low and beat $1^1/_2$ minutes. Stop and scrape bowl.

2 Reduce speed to low and add eggs, 1 at a time, mixing 15 seconds after each addition. Turn to medium-low and beat 30 seconds. Reduce speed to low and quickly add nuts; mix about 15 seconds more.

3 Pour batter into greased and floured 10-inch bundt pan. Bake at 350°F for 60 to 65 minutes. Cool in pan 10 minutes, and then remove and cool on wire racks.

# Double Lemon Cake Roll

## Cake

- 4 eggs
- 3/4 cup granulated sugar
- 1/4 cup water
- 1/2 teaspoon vanilla
- 1/2 teaspoon lemon extract
- 2/3 cup all–purpose flour
- 1 teaspoon baking powder
- 1/4 teaspoon salt

## Lemon Filling

- 1 package (8 ounces) light cream cheese, softened
- 1 cup powdered sugar
- 1 tablespoon lemon juice
- 2 teaspoons grated lemon peel

*Makes 10 servings (1-inch slice per serving)*

1. To make cake, beat eggs in bowl of electric stand mixer on high about 3 minutes or until very thick and lemon-colored. Continuing on high, gradually add sugar, beating about 1 minute. Stop and scrape bowl.

2. Add water, vanilla and lemon extract. Turn to medium and beat about 30 seconds. Continuing on medium, gradually add flour, baking powder and salt. Beat about 30 seconds or until batter is smooth.

3. Line a 15 1/2 × 10 1/2 × 1-inch baking pan with waxed paper, foil or parchment paper. Grease well. Pour batter into pan, spreading to corners. Bake at 375°F for 11 to 13 minutes or until toothpick inserted into center comes out clean. Remove from oven and immediately turn onto a towel sprinkled with powdered sugar. Remove paper or foil. Roll cake and towel together, starting on short side. Cool completely on wire rack.

4. Meanwhile, to make lemon filling, beat together all ingredients in bowl of electric stand mixer on medium about 1 1/2 minutes or until well mixed.

5. When completely cool, unroll cake and spread with lemon filling. Reroll and sprinkle with powdered sugar. Serve immediately.

# Double Chocolate Pound Cake

## Pound Cake

- 3 cups all-purpose flour
- 2 cups granulated sugar
- 1/2 cup unsweetened Dutch-processed cocoa powder
- 3 teaspoons baking powder
- 1/2 teaspoon salt
- 1 cup butter, softened
- 1 1/4 cups low-fat (1%) milk
- 1 teaspoon vanilla
- 5 eggs

## Chocolate Glaze

- 2 squares (1 ounce each) unsweetened chocolate
- 3 tablespoons butter
- 1 cup powdered sugar
- 3/4 teaspoon vanilla
- 2 tablespoons hot water

*Makes 16 servings*

1 Combine dry ingredients in bowl of electric stand mixer. Add butter, milk and vanilla. Turn to low and mix about 1 minute. Stop and scrape bowl. Increase speed to medium and beat about 2 minutes. Stop and scrape bowl. Reduce speed to low and add eggs, 1 at a time, mixing about 15 seconds after each addition. Turn to medium-low and beat about 30 seconds.

2 Pour batter into greased and floured 10-inch tube pan. Bake at 325°F for 1 hour 20 minutes or until toothpick inserted into center comes out clean. Cool completely on wire rack. Remove cake from pan.

3 To make chocolate glaze, melt chocolate and butter in small saucepan over low heat. Remove from heat. Stir in powdered sugar and vanilla. Stir in water, 1 teaspoon at a time, until glaze is of desired consistency. Drizzle cake with chocolate glaze.

# Orange Chiffon Cake

2¼ cups cake flour

1½ cups sugar

3 teaspoons baking powder

1 teaspoon salt

½ cup vegetable oil

5 egg yolks, at room temperature

3 tablespoons grated orange peel

¾ cup orange juice

8 egg whites, at room temperature

½ teaspoon cream of tartar

Orange Glaze (recipe follows)

**TIP**

*Cut angel, chiffon or sponge cakes with a long serrated knife, using a gentle sawing motion; or use a cake breaker.*

*Makes 1 cake*

1 Sift flour, sugar, baking powder and salt into bowl of electric stand mixer. Make well in center and add oil, egg yolks and orange peel. Mix on low until ingredients are moistened. Stop and scrape bowl. Add orange juice and beat on medium-high 1 minute. Set aside.

2 Place egg whites and cream of tartar in clean, dry, large bowl. Beat with mixer on high until dry. Fold batter into egg whites until just blended.

3 Pour batter into ungreased 10-inch tube pan. Bake at 325°F for 55 minutes. Increase oven to 350°F and bake 10 minutes longer or until pick inserted near center of cake is clean when removed. Remove cake from oven and invert to cool.

4 To remove from pan, gently loosen all edges with blade of thin knife. Place on serving plate and drizzle Orange Glaze over top.

## Orange Glaze

*Makes about ½ cup*

½ cup orange juice

4 to 5 tablespoons sugar

Place orange juice and sugar in small saucepan. Bring to a boil over medium heat and stir until slightly thickened. Remove from heat and cool.

Chocolate Chip Shortbread with Earl Grey-Infused Glaze *(recipe on page 108)*

# cookies, bars, and candies

There comes a time in every week (or maybe every day) when nothing is more satisfying than a snack of fresh-from-the-oven cookies alongside a cool and creamy glass of milk.

The following collection of recipes not only will help you master the classics, but will also push you to expand upon your repertoire of mouthwatering brownies, cookies, and other sweets.

# Chocolate Chip Shortbread
## with Earl Grey-Infused Glaze

*(photo on page 106)*

1 cup unsalted butter

1/2 cup sugar

1 teaspoon grated orange peel

2 cups all-purpose flour

1/4 cup cornstarch

1/4 teaspoon salt

1/2 cup chocolate chips

Earl Grey-Infused Glaze
(recipe follows)

### TIP

*For optimal flavor, use unsalted butter to allow the flavors of butter, chocolate, orange and tea to stand out.*

*Makes 32 shortbread*

1 Preheat oven to 300°F. Mix butter, sugar and orange peel in bowl of electric stand mixer on low until combined. Continuing on low, gradually mix in flour, cornstarch and salt. When dough has formed, mix in chocolate chips.

2 Roll dough into 1/4-inch-thick rectangle on lightly floured board. Cut dough lengthwise into 4 rows and diagonally into 8 rows. Place shortbread 1 inch apart on ungreased baking sheet.

3 Bake 25 to 30 minutes or until bottoms begin to brown. Cool 5 minutes. Remove from pan; cool completely on wire rack. Prepare Earl Grey-Infused Glaze. Drizzle over shortbread.

## Earl Grey-Infused Glaze

*Makes 1/3 cup or enough to drizzle 32 shortbread*

1/4 cup boiling water

3 bags Earl Grey tea

1 cup powdered sugar

1 tablespoon butter, softened

Pour boiling water over tea bags; let steep 3 to 5 minutes. Remove tea bags.

In small bowl, stir together powdered sugar and butter. Gradually stir in enough tea to make glaze thin enough to drizzle.

| **cookies, bars, and candies**

# Chocolate Chip Blondies

½ cup plus 2 tablespoons butter

2 cups packed brown sugar

2 eggs

1½ teaspoons vanilla

2 cups all-purpose flour

1½ teaspoons baking powder

½ teaspoon salt

½ cup chopped walnuts

¼ cup semisweet chocolate chips

*Makes 2 dozen bars*

1 Preheat oven to 350°F. Grease and flour 13×9×2-inch pan. Place butter, brown sugar, eggs and vanilla in bowl of electric stand mixer. Turn to medium-low and mix 1 minute. Stop and scrape bowl.

2 Add flour, baking powder and salt. Turn to low and mix 15 seconds. Stop and scrape bowl. Continue mixing on low, and add nuts and chocolate chips, mixing just until combined.

3 Press dough into prepared pan. Bake 20 to 25 minutes. Cool in pan, and then cut into 3×1½-inch bars.

**cookies, bars, and candies** |

# Coconut-Lemon Layer Bars

2 cups vanilla wafer crumbs

6 tablespoons butter, melted

1 package (8 ounces) cream cheese, softened

1 tablespoon grated lemon peel

3 tablespoons lemon juice

1 egg

1 cup (about 6 ounces) white chocolate chips

1 cup sweetened flaked coconut

1/2 cup chopped macadamia nuts

*Makes 32 bars*

1 Preheat oven to 350°F. Stir together vanilla wafer crumbs and butter in medium bowl. Press crumb mixture firmly in bottom of 13×9-inch baking pan.

2 Place cream cheese, lemon peel, lemon juice and egg in bowl of electric stand mixer. Beat on medium-low until smooth. Spread evenly over crumb mixture.

3 Layer evenly with chips, coconut and nuts; press down firmly with fork.

4 Bake 25 to 30 minutes or until lightly browned. Cool completely. Cut into 4 rows by 8 rows. Cover and refrigerate until ready to serve.

# Macadamia Chocolate Chunk **Cookies**

1 cup firmly packed brown sugar

³/₄ cup granulated sugar

1 cup (2 sticks) butter, softened

2 teaspoons vanilla

2 eggs

2¹/₂ cups all-purpose flour, divided

¹/₂ cup unsweetened cocoa powder

1 teaspoon baking powder

¹/₂ teaspoon salt

1 package (8 ounces) semisweet baking chocolate, cut into small chunks

1 jar (3¹/₂ ounces) macadamia nuts, coarsely chopped

*Makes 4 dozen cookies*

1 Place brown sugar, granulated sugar, butter, vanilla and eggs in bowl of electric stand mixer. Turn to low and mix about 30 seconds. Stop and scrape bowl. Turn to medium-low and beat about 1 minute. Stop and scrape bowl.

2 Add 1 cup flour, cocoa powder, baking powder and salt. Turn to low and mix about 30 seconds. Gradually add remaining 1¹/₂ cups flour and mix 30 seconds longer. Increase speed to medium-low and mix about 30 seconds. Reduce speed to low and add chocolate chunks and nuts, mixing just until blended.

3 Drop by rounded teaspoonfuls onto greased baking sheets about 2 inches apart. Bake at 325°F for 12 to 13 minutes or until edges are set. Do not overbake. Cool on baking sheets about 1 minute. Remove to wire racks and cool completely.

# Double-Decker Butterscotch Brownies

³/₄ cup (1¹/₂ sticks) butter

2 cups sugar

2 teaspoons vanilla

3 eggs

³/₄ cup unsweetened cocoa

1 cup all-purpose flour

Butterscotch Glaze
(recipe follows)

Chocolate Ganache
(recipe follows)

*Makes 2 dozen bars*

1 Mix butter, sugar and vanilla in bowl of electric stand mixer on low about 30 seconds or until sugar is incorporated. Turn mixer to medium-high and beat until creamy, about 2 minutes. Stop and scrape bowl. Turn to medium and add eggs, 1 at a time, beating about 15 seconds after each addition. Stop and scrape bowl. Add cocoa and flour. Turn to low and mix just until blended, about 30 seconds.

2 Pour into 15¹/₂ × 10¹/₂-inch jelly-roll pan that has been lined with foil and greased. Bake at 350°F for 14 to 16 minutes or until top springs back when touched lightly in the center. Remove from oven and cool in pan 2 minutes. Invert onto cutting board, remove foil and flip right-side up onto wire rack; cool completely.

3 While brownies cool, prepare Butterscotch Glaze. Pour glaze onto brownies and spread evenly. Before glaze sets, slice brownie layer in half and stack one half on the other. Cool until glaze sets. Drizzle with Chocolate Ganache. Slice into 2 × 1³/₄-inch bars once ganache sets.

## Butterscotch Glaze

1 package (about 11 ounces) butterscotch-flavored baking chips

¹/₄ cup water

¹/₄ cup sugar

1 tablespoon light corn syrup

Place butterscotch chips in bowl of electric stand mixer. Bring water, sugar and corn syrup to boil in small saucepan over medium-high heat. Set mixer to low and carefully pour in hot syrup. Mix until smooth. Cool slightly but use while still warm; mixture sets as it cools.

**cookies, bars, and candies**

# Chocolate Ganache

½ **cup whipping cream**
1 **cup chocolate chips**

Heat cream in small saucepan over medium-low heat until bubbles appear around edge of pan. Pour over chocolate chips and stir constantly until mixture is smooth and begins to thicken. Use while warm; mixture thickens and sets as it cools.

**cookies, bars, and candies**

# Peanut Butter Cookies

½ cup peanut butter

½ cup butter, softened

½ cup granulated sugar

½ cup packed brown sugar

1 egg

½ teaspoon vanilla

½ teaspoon baking soda

¼ teaspoon salt

1¼ cups all-purpose flour

*Makes 3 dozen cookies*

1 Place peanut butter and butter in bowl of electric stand mixer. Turn to medium and beat until mixture is smooth, about 1 minute. Stop and scrape bowl. Add sugars, egg and vanilla. Reduce speed to medium-low and beat about 1 minute. Stop and scrape bowl.

2 Turn mixer to low. Gradually add all remaining ingredients to sugar mixture and mix about 30 seconds. Turn to medium-low and mix about 30 seconds.

3 Roll dough into 1-inch balls. Place about 2 inches apart on ungreased baking sheets. Press flat with fork in crisscross pattern to ¼-inch thickness.

4 Bake at 375°F until golden brown, about 10 to 12 minutes. Remove from baking sheets immediately and cool on wire racks.

# Fudge Brownies

1 cup (2 sticks) butter, softened, divided

4 squares (1 ounce each) unsweetened chocolate

2 cups sugar

1 teaspoon vanilla

3 eggs

1 cup all-purpose flour

1/2 teaspoon salt

1 cup chopped walnuts or pecans

*Makes 2 dozen bars*

1 Melt 1/2 cup butter and chocolate in small saucepan over low heat; set aside to cool.

2 Place remaining 1/2 cup butter, sugar and vanilla in bowl of electric stand mixer. Turn to low and mix about 30 seconds. Turn to medium and beat about 2 minutes. Turn to medium-low. Add eggs, 1 at a time, beating about 15 seconds after each addition. Stop and scrape bowl.

3 Add cooled chocolate mixture to mixer bowl. Turn to low and mix about 30 seconds. Stop and scrape bowl. Add all remaining ingredients. Turn to low and mix until well blended, about 30 seconds.

4 Pour into greased and floured 13×9×2-inch baking pan. Bake at 350°F for 45 minutes. Cool in pan on wire rack.

**cookies, bars, and candies** |

# Chocolate Fudge

Butter

2 cups sugar

1/8 teaspoon salt

3/4 cup evaporated milk

1 teaspoon light corn syrup

2 squares (1 ounce each)
   semisweet chocolate

2 tablespoons butter

1 teaspoon vanilla

2 cups chopped walnuts or
   pecans

*Makes about 5 dozen candies*

1 Butter sides of heavy 2-quart saucepan. Combine sugar, salt, evaporated milk, corn syrup and chocolate in pan. Cook and stir over medium heat until chocolate melts and sugar dissolves. Cook to soft ball stage (236°F) without stirring. Remove immediately from heat. Add butter without stirring. Cool to lukewarm (110°F). Stir in vanilla.

2 Pour mixture into bowl of electric stand mixer. Turn to medium-low and mix about 8 minutes or until fudge stiffens and loses its gloss. Quickly turn to low and add walnuts, mixing just until blended. Spread in buttered 9×9×2-inch baking pan. Cool at room temperature. Cut into 1-inch squares when firm.

# Melt-in-Your-Mouth Macaroons

1 can (8 ounces) almond paste

2 egg whites

1/2 cup granulated sugar

1 cup powdered sugar

*Makes 2 dozen cookies*

1 Place almond paste and egg whites in bowl of electric stand mixer. Turn to medium-low and beat 1 minute. Stop and scrape bowl.

2 Add granulated sugar. Turn to medium-low and beat 30 seconds. Stop and scrape bowl. Sift powdered sugar into bowl. Turn mixer to medium and beat 15 seconds.

3 Drop dough by teaspoonfuls 2 inches apart onto greased and floured baking sheets. Bake at 350°F for 12 to 15 minutes. Cool on wire racks.

# Chocolate Chip Cookies

1 cup granulated sugar

1 cup packed brown sugar

1 cup (2 sticks) butter, softened

2 eggs

1½ teaspoons vanilla

1 teaspoon baking soda

1 teaspoon salt

3 cups all-purpose flour

12 ounces semisweet chocolate chips

*Makes 4½ dozen cookies*

1 Preheat oven to 375°F. Place sugars, butter, eggs and vanilla in bowl of electric stand mixer. Turn to low and mix about 30 seconds. Stop and scrape bowl. Turn to medium-low and beat about 30 seconds. Stop and scrape bowl.

2 Mix baking soda, salt and flour in separate bowl. Turn mixer to low. Gradually add flour mixture to sugar mixture and mix about 2 minutes. Turn to medium-low and mix about 30 seconds. Stop and scrape bowl. Add chocolate chips. Turn to low and mix about 15 seconds.

3 Drop dough by rounded teaspoonfuls onto greased baking sheets about 2 inches apart. Bake 10 to 12 minutes. Remove from baking sheets immediately. Cool on wire racks.

**cookies, bars, and candies** |

# Cocoa Bottom Banana Pecan Bars

1 cup sugar

½ cup (1 stick) butter, softened

5 ripe bananas, mashed

1 egg

1 teaspoon vanilla

1½ cups all-purpose flour

1 teaspoon baking powder

1 teaspoon baking soda

½ teaspoon salt

½ cup chopped pecans

¼ cup unsweetened cocoa powder

*Makes about 1½ dozen bars*

1 Preheat oven to 350°F. Grease 13×9-inch baking pan. Beat sugar and butter in bowl of electric stand mixer at medium until creamy. Add bananas, egg and vanilla; beat until well blended. Combine flour, baking powder, baking soda and salt in medium bowl. Add flour mixture to banana mixture; beat until well blended. Stir in pecans.

2 Divide batter in half. Stir cocoa into one half. Spread chocolate batter into prepared pan. Top with plain batter; swirl with knife.

3 Bake 30 to 35 minutes or until edges are lightly browned. Cool completely in pan on wire rack. Cut into bars.

| cookies, bars, and candies

# Divinity

3 cups sugar

³/₄ cup light corn syrup

¹/₂ cup water

2 egg whites

1 teaspoon almond extract

1 cup chopped walnuts or pecans

*Makes about 3¹/₂ dozen candies*

**1** Place sugar, corn syrup and water in heavy saucepan. Cook and stir over medium heat to hard ball stage (248°F). Remove from heat and let stand until temperature drops to 220°F; do not stir.

**2** Place egg whites in bowl of electric stand mixer. Turn to high and whip until soft peaks form, about 1 minute. Gradually add syrup mixture in fine stream and whip about 2¹/₂ minutes longer.

**3** Reduce speed to medium-low. Add almond extract and whip until mixture starts to become dry, 20 to 25 minutes. Turn to low and add walnuts, mixing just until blended.

**4** Drop mixture by tablespoonfuls onto waxed paper or greased baking sheet to form patties.

**cookies, bars, and candies** |

# Primo Pumpkin **Brownies**

¾ cup packed brown sugar

½ cup (1 stick) unsalted butter, softened

1 teaspoon vanilla

1 egg

1⅓ cups all-purpose flour

1 cup solid-pack canned pumpkin

2 teaspoons pumpkin pie spice*

1 teaspoon baking powder

¼ teaspoon salt

½ cup toffee baking bits

White Chocolate Cream Cheese Frosting (recipe follows)

*Substitute 1 teaspoon ground cinnamon, ½ teaspoon ground ginger and ¼ teaspoon each ground allspice and ground nutmeg for 2 teaspoons pumpkin pie spice.*

*Makes 9 brownies*

1 Preheat oven to 350°F. Grease 8-inch square baking pan. Place brown sugar, butter and vanilla in bowl of electric stand mixer. Turn to medium and beat until smooth. Add egg; beat until fluffy. Stir in flour, pumpkin, pumpkin pie spice, baking powder and salt. Fold in toffee bits. Spread evenly in prepared pan.

2 Bake 40 to 45 minutes or until toothpick inserted near center comes out clean. Cool completely in pan on wire rack.

3 Prepare White Chocolate Cream Cheese Frosting. Frost brownies; cut into squares.

## White Chocolate Cream Cheese Frosting

*Makes about 2 cups*

2 tablespoons whipping cream

4 squares (1 ounce each) white chocolate, chopped

6 ounces cream cheese, softened

⅓ cup powdered sugar, sifted

1 Heat cream in small saucepan over medium heat until almost boiling; remove from heat. Add white chocolate; stir until completely melted. Cool slightly.

2 Beat cream cheese and sugar in bowl of electric stand mixer at medium 1 minute or until fluffy. Beat in chocolate mixture until smooth.

# Raisin-Apricot Oatmeal Cookies

½ cup butter
½ cup shortening
2 teaspoons vanilla
¾ cup granulated sugar
¼ cup packed brown sugar
2 eggs
2 cups quick oats
1½ cups all-purpose flour
1 teaspoon baking soda
½ teaspoon salt
¾ cup raisins
½ cup chopped dried apricots

*Makes 4 dozen cookies*

1 Place butter, shortening, vanilla, sugars and eggs in bowl of electric stand mixer. Turn mixer to low and mix about 30 seconds. Stop and scrape bowl. Turn to medium-low and beat about 30 seconds. Stop and scrape bowl. Add oats, flour, baking soda, salt, raisins and apricots. Turn to low and mix about 30 seconds more.

2 Drop dough by rounded teaspoonfuls onto greased baking sheets. Bake at 375°F for 8 to 10 minutes or until light golden brown.

**Cookies for the freezer:** Double the ingredients and prepare in 6-quart mixer bowl. Enjoy cookies now and freeze some for later. Makes 96 cookies.

# Ultimate Sugar Cookies

1 cup butter, softened
1 teaspoon vanilla
¾ cup sugar
2 eggs, beaten
1 teaspoon cream of tartar
½ teaspoon baking soda
¼ teaspoon ground nutmeg
¼ teaspoon salt
2 cups all-purpose flour
Sugar

*Makes 4 dozen cookies*

1 Place butter and vanilla in bowl of electric stand mixer. Turn mixer to medium and beat about 2 minutes or until mixture is smooth. Gradually add ¾ cup sugar and beat about 1½ minutes longer. Add eggs and beat about 30 seconds. Stop and scrape bowl.

2 Turn mixer to low. Gradually add cream of tartar, baking soda, nutmeg, salt and flour to sugar mixture. Mix until well blended, about 1 minute.

3 Drop dough by rounded teaspoonfuls onto greased baking sheets about 3 inches apart. Bake at 400°F for 6 to 8 minutes. Sprinkle with additional sugar while still hot. Remove from baking sheets immediately and cool on wire racks.

**cookies, bars, and candies**

# Dulce de Leche Blondies

2 cups all-purpose flour

1 teaspoon baking soda

1 teaspoon salt

1 cup (2 sticks) butter, softened

1 cup packed brown sugar

2 eggs

1½ teaspoons vanilla

1 (14-ounce) package caramels

½ cup evaporated milk

*Makes about 3 dozen bars*

1 Preheat oven to 350°F. Grease 13×9-inch baking pan. Sift flour, baking soda and salt into medium bowl; set aside.

2 Beat butter and brown sugar in bowl of electric stand mixer until creamy. Add eggs and vanilla; beat until smooth. Gradually stir in flour mixture. Spread half of batter in prepared pan. Bake about 8 minutes; cool 5 minutes on wire rack.

3 Meanwhile, melt caramels with evaporated milk in nonstick saucepan over very low heat; reserve 2 tablespoons. Pour remaining caramel mixture over baked bottom layer. Drop tablespoonfuls of remaining batter over caramel layer; swirl slightly with knife.

4 Bake 25 minutes or until golden brown. Cool completely in pan on wire rack. Cut into squares. Reheat reserved caramel, if necessary; drizzle over bars.

Chocolate Chili and Orange Fondue *(recipe on page 128)*

# desserts

When hosting a swanky dinner soirée or bringing a dish to a potluck, nothing makes a better final statement than a luscious homemade dessert.

Each of the following recipes combines decadent flavors with stunning presentation to create the ultimate grand finale. From fondue to layered tortes, these divine desserts are the perfect finishing touch to any meal.

# Chocolate Chili
# and Orange Fondue

*(photo on page 126)*

- 2 (4-ounce) 60 to 70% bittersweet chocolate bars, coarsely chopped
- 2 tablespoons butter, softened
- 1½ cups (12 ounces) heavy or whipping cream
- ½ cup frozen orange juice concentrate, thawed but not diluted
- 1 teaspoon vanilla
- ½ teaspoon ancho or chipotle chili powder

*Makes 6 servings*

1 Place chopped chocolate and butter in medium bowl; set aside.

2 Heat cream in small saucepan until boiling; pour over chocolate. Stir in orange juice concentrate, vanilla and chili powder. Mix until chocolate is melted and mixture is smooth. Serve immediately in individual bowls or fondue pot.

3 Serve fondue alongside an assortment of dippers that may include strawberries, orange segments, apple slices, pear slices, pineapple chunks, banana chunks, cookies, marshmallows, pound cake cubes and large pretzel rods.

# Pots de Crème au Chocolat

2 cups heavy cream

1 tablespoon sugar

4 squares (1 ounce each)
semisweet chocolate,
melted

5 egg yolks

*Makes 6 servings*

1 Heat cream and sugar in double boiler over boiling water, stirring constantly, until sugar is dissolved. Add chocolate and stir until well blended. Remove from heat and set aside.

2 Place egg yolks in bowl of electric stand mixer. Turn to medium-high, and whip 1 minute. Reduce to low; gradually add cream mixture, whipping until well blended.

3 Fill 6 (6-ounce) custard cups or crème pots two-thirds full. Place cups in 13×9×2-inch pan. Pour boiling water to fill pan 1½ inches deep. Bake at 325°F until firm, 20 to 25 minutes. Chill at least 2 hours.

# Chocolate Peanut Torte

3/4 cup butter, softened

3/4 cup sugar

6 ounces almond paste

5 eggs

2/3 cup graham cracker crumbs

3/4 cup all-purpose flour

3/4 teaspoon baking powder

1 1/3 cups ground peanuts

Chocolate Peanut Frosting
(recipe follows)

*Makes 1 torte*

1 Place butter, sugar and almond paste in bowl of electric stand mixer. Beat on medium 1 minute. With mixer running, add eggs, 1 at a time, beating 15 seconds after each addition. Stop and scrape bowl.

2 Reduce speed to medium-low and gradually add graham cracker crumbs, flour and baking powder; beat 1 minute more. Stir in peanuts, mixing just until blended.

3 Pour batter into 9-inch springform pan that has been lined with waxed paper and greased. Bake at 350°F for 50 to 55 minutes.

4 Remove from pan and cool on wire rack. When cool, slice cake in thirds to form 3 layers. Frost with Chocolate Peanut Frosting.

## Chocolate Peanut Frosting

1/2 cup butter, softened

1/2 cup powdered sugar

2 ounces almond paste

1 1/3 cups creamy peanut butter

4 squares (1 ounce each) semisweet chocolate, melted

Place butter, powdered sugar and almond paste in bowl of electric stand mixer. Beat on medium 2 minutes or until creamy. Stop and scrape bowl.

Add peanut butter and chocolate. Turn to medium-high and beat 2 minutes or until fluffy.

# Double Chocolate Mousse
## with Raspberry Sauce

6 ounces bittersweet
   chocolate, chopped
   into $3/4$-inch chunks

6 ounces white chocolate,
   chopped into $3/4$-inch
   chunks

2 cups whipping cream

   Raspberry Sauce (recipe
   follows)

*Makes 6 servings ($2/3$ cup mousse and $1/4$ cup raspberry sauce per serving)*

1 Place bittersweet chocolate in 1 (3- to 4-cup) microwaveable bowl. Place white chocolate in second microwaveable bowl. Cover each with waxed paper. Place 1 bowl at a time in microwave oven and heat on HIGH $1^1/2$ minutes. Stop and stir. If chocolate is not melted, repeat process 30 seconds at a time or until melted. Stop and stir.

2 Heat cream in heavy saucepan over medium heat until very hot, but do not boil. Remove from heat. Pour 1 cup cream into each chocolate bowl. Stir each until completely mixed. Cover bowls; refrigerate about 2 hours.

3 Pour white chocolate mixture into bowl of electric stand mixer. Gradually turn speed to medium; beat 4 to $4^1/2$ minutes or until soft peaks form. Spoon about $1/3$ cup mixture into each of 6 stemmed dessert dishes. Set aside.

4 Pour bittersweet chocolate mixture into mixer bowl. Gradually turn speed to medium; beat about 3 minutes or until soft peaks form. Spoon about $1/3$ cup mixture over white chocolate layer. Cover dishes with plastic wrap or foil. Refrigerate 8 hours or overnight.

# Raspberry Sauce

1 package (14 to 16 ounces) frozen unsweetened raspberries, thawed

¹⁄₄ cup water

¹⁄₄ cup sugar

1 tablespoon cornstarch

Place raspberries in blender container. Cover and blend until smooth. Pour mixture into wire mesh strainer over small saucepan; press with back of spoon to squeeze out liquid. Discard seeds and pulp in strainer.

Add remaining ingredients to saucepan. Cook over medium heat, stirring constantly, until thickened and bubbly. Remove from heat and cool. Store sauce in covered container in refrigerator. Stir before using.

Spoon Raspberry Sauce over chocolate in dessert dishes before serving.

# Individual Irish Coffee
# Baked Alaska

2 cups vanilla ice cream, softened

2 cups coffee ice cream, softened

### Cake

2/3 cup sugar

3 eggs, separated

1/3 cup all-purpose flour

1/3 cup unsweetened cocoa powder

1/4 cup cornstarch

2 tablespoons Irish cream-flavored liqueur

### Meringue

4 egg whites

1/2 cup sugar

3 tablespoons whiskey

*Makes 4 servings*

1 Preheat oven to 350°F. Line 4 (1-cup) ramekins with plastic wrap. Place 1/2 cup vanilla ice cream in each ramekin. Top with 1/2 cup coffee ice cream. Fold plastic down on top of ice cream. Freeze 4 hours or until firm.

2 For Cake, line 13×9-inch baking pan with waxed paper. Beat sugar and egg yolks in medium bowl of electric stand mixer on high 4 minutes or until pale and thick; set aside. Clean bowl. Place egg whites in mixer bowl and beat on high until stiff but not until dry peaks form. Sift flour, cocoa and cornstarch into yolk mixture; stir gently until blended. Fold in egg whites. Carefully spread mixture into prepared baking pan.

3 Bake 10 minutes or until cake springs back lightly when touched. Cool completely in pan on wire rack. Cut cake into 3-inch rounds with cookie or biscuit cutter. Place rounds on top of ice cream in ramekins. Brush rounds with liqueur. Freeze until ready to top with meringue.

4 For Meringue, preheat oven to 525°F. Beat egg whites in clean mixer bowl on high until foamy. Slowly add sugar, beating until stiff, glossy peaks form.

5 Remove desserts from ramekins using plastic wrap. Discard plastic wrap. Place desserts, cake-side down, on baking sheet. Spread $^2/_3$ cup meringue over each dessert, working quickly to prevent ice cream from melting. Bake 2 minutes or until meringue is golden.

6 Heat whiskey in small skillet over low heat 1 minute. Do not boil. Using long-handled match, ignite whiskey. Carefully pour over each dessert. Allow whiskey to burn out; serve immediately.

# Almond Dacquoise

6 ounces blanched almonds, ground

1 cup powdered sugar

1 1/2 tablespoons cornstarch

6 egg whites

1/8 teaspoon salt

1/4 teaspoon cream of tartar

3 tablespoons sugar

1 1/4 teaspoons vanilla

1/4 teaspoon almond extract

Chocolate Buttercream Filling (recipe follows)

*Makes 1 (8-inch) cake*

1 Combine almonds, powdered sugar and cornstarch; set aside. Place egg whites in bowl of electric stand mixer. Turn to medium and whip until foamy. Add salt and cream of tartar and continue whipping until soft peaks form. Sprinkle in sugar, vanilla and almond extract, beating until stiff peaks form. Reduce to low and quickly add almond mixture, mixing just until blended.

2 Using a pastry bag fitted with large (1/2-inch) plain tip, pipe mixture onto greased and floured baking sheets to form 3 (8-inch) circles. Bake at 250°F for 35 to 45 minutes. Remove from baking sheets and cool on foil. Fill and frost with Chocolate Buttercream Filling.

## Chocolate Buttercream Filling

2 egg yolks

1 cup powdered sugar

2 squares (1 ounce each) semisweet chocolate, melted

3/4 cup (1 1/2 sticks) butter, softened

1/2 teaspoon vanilla

Place egg yolks in bowl of electric stand mixer. Turn to medium and whip 2 minutes. Stop and scrape bowl.

Turn to medium-low and gradually add powdered sugar, chocolate, butter and vanilla; continue beating until fluffy, about 5 minutes.

# Lemon Soufflé

2 tablespoons butter

$^1/_3$ cup plus 3 tablespoons sugar, divided

2 tablespoons grated lemon peel

3 tablespoons all-purpose flour

$^3/_4$ cup milk

$^1/_3$ cup freshly squeezed lemon juice

5 eggs, separated

*Makes 6 servings*

1 Grease 1$^1/_2$-quart soufflé dish with 1 tablespoon butter. Combine 3 tablespoons sugar and 1 tablespoon lemon peel in small bowl. Sprinkle soufflé dish with mixture; set aside.

2 Melt remaining butter in saucepan over medium heat. Add flour and blend well; cook 1 minute. Gradually add milk, stirring until smooth. Add remaining sugar and bring to a boil, stirring constantly for 30 seconds. Add lemon juice and remaining lemon peel. Place mixture in bowl of electric stand mixer. Turn to medium-low and beat 1 minute. Stop and scrape bowl. Turn to medium and add egg yolks, 1 at a time, beating 15 seconds after each addition. Remove from bowl and set aside. Clean bowl.

3 Place egg whites in mixer bowl. Turn to medium-high and whip until stiff but not dry. Gently fold egg yolk mixture into egg whites. Pour into soufflé dish. Run knife around soufflé dish inserted 1$^1/_2$ inches deep and 1 inch from edge.

4 Place soufflé dish in 13×9×2-inch pan and add boiling water 1 inch in depth. Bake at 350°F for 25 to 30 minutes. Serve immediately.

# Pineapple Frozen Yogurt

$^1/_4$ cup egg substitute

$^1/_4$ cup sugar

$^1/_2$ cup fat-free half-and-half

$^1/_2$ cup plain reduced-fat yogurt

$^3/_4$ cup crushed pineapple in juice

*Makes 4 servings (1 pint)*

1 Beat egg substitute and sugar together until thick and cream-colored. Add half-and-half, yogurt and pineapple; mix well. Chill mixture completely before adding to ice cream maker.

2 Follow manufacturer's directions for using ice cream maker, or pour mixture into shallow glass baking dish and place in freezer. Every 10 minutes, stir and scrape mixture with rubber spatula until it reaches desired consistency, about 1 hour.

3 Scoop out 1 or 2 ($^1/_2$-cup) servings, returning unused portion to freezer in covered container.

# French Vanilla Ice Cream

2½ cups half-and-half
8 egg yolks
1 cup sugar
2½ cups whipping cream
4 teaspoons vanilla
⅛ teaspoon salt

*Makes 16 servings (½ cup per serving)*

1 In medium saucepan over medium heat, heat half-and-half until very hot but not boiling, stirring often. Remove from heat; set aside.

2 Place egg yolks and sugar in large bowl of electric stand mixer. Mix on low about 1 minute or until well blended and slightly thickened. Continuing on low, very gradually add warm half-and-half; mix until blended. Return mixture to same saucepan; cook over medium heat until small bubbles form around edge and mixture is steamy, stirring constantly. Do not boil. Transfer mixture to large bowl; stir in whipping cream, vanilla and salt. Cover and chill thoroughly, at least 8 hours. Freeze in ice cream maker following manufacturer's directions. Immediately transfer ice cream to serving dishes or freeze in airtight container.

## Fresh Strawberry Ice Cream

In medium bowl, combine 2 cups chopped, fresh strawberries (or other fresh fruit) and 2 to 3 teaspoons sugar, if desired. Let stand while ice cream is processing. Add during last 3 to 5 minutes of freeze time. Makes 20 servings (½ cup per serving).

## Cookies and Cream Ice Cream

Add 1½ cups chopped, cream-filled chocolate sandwich cookies (or other cookies, nuts or candies) during last 1 to 2 minutes of freeze time. Makes 19 servings (½ cup per serving).

# Triple Chocolate Ice Cream

2 cups whipping cream, divided

2 squares (1 ounce each) semisweet baking chocolate, coarsely chopped

2 squares (1 ounce each) unsweetened baking chocolate, coarsely chopped

2 cups half-and-half

1 cup sugar

$1/3$ cup unsweetened cocoa powder

8 egg yolks

4 teaspoons vanilla

$1/8$ teaspoon salt

4 bars (1.55 ounces each) milk chocolate, chopped (about $1^{1}/_{2}$ cups)

*Makes 16 servings ($^{1}/_{2}$ cup per serving)*

1 In small saucepan, place $^{1}/_{2}$ cup whipping cream, semisweet chocolate and unsweetened chocolate. Heat over medium-low heat until chocolate melts, stirring frequently. Remove from heat; set aside. In medium saucepan over medium heat, heat half-and-half until very hot but not boiling, stirring often. Remove from heat; set aside.

2 In small bowl, combine sugar and cocoa powder; set aside. Place egg yolks in bowl of electric stand mixer. Turn to low and gradually add sugar mixture; mix about 30 seconds or until well blended and slightly thickened. Continuing on low, very gradually add chocolate mixture and half-and-half; mix until well blended.

3 Return half-and-half mixture to medium saucepan. Cook, stirring constantly, over medium heat until small bubbles form around edge and mixture is steamy. Do not boil. Transfer half-and-half mixture to large bowl; stir in remaining $1^{1}/_{2}$ cups whipping cream, vanilla and salt. Cover and chill thoroughly, at least 8 hours.

4 Attach freeze bowl to mixer according to manufacturer's instructions, and transfer ice cream to mixer. Mix on low 10 to 15 minutes or until desired consistency. Add milk chocolate during last 1 to 2 minutes of freeze time. Immediately transfer ice cream into serving dishes, or freeze in an airtight container.

# Almond Petit Fours

1 1/2  cups all-purpose flour

1/3  cup ground almonds

1/2  teaspoon baking powder

1/2  teaspoon baking soda

1/2  teaspoon salt

1/2  cup (1 stick) butter, softened

1  cup sugar

1  teaspoon almond extract

2  eggs

3/4  cup buttermilk

1/2  cup seedless raspberry jam

Petit Four Icing (recipe follows)

Assorted decorations such as multicolored decorator sprinkles, chocolate shavings, silver dragées, etc.

*Makes 48 petit fours*

1 Preheat oven to 350°F. Grease and flour 13×9-inch rectangular pan. Stir together flour, almonds, baking powder, baking soda and salt; set aside.

2 Beat butter, sugar and almond extract together in bowl of electric stand mixer on medium 2 minutes, scraping bowl occasionally. Mix in eggs on low until combined.

3 Mix in flour mixture alternately with buttermilk on low in 3 additions, scraping bowl occasionally. Spread evenly in prepared pan.

4 Bake 25 to 30 minutes or until cake springs back when lightly touched. Cool in pan 10 minutes. Loosen edges and invert onto rack to cool completely. Slice cake in half horizontally. Spread jam over cut side of cake. Place top layer of cake over jam-covered bottom layer.

5 Make Petit Four Icing. While icing sugar mixture cooks, cut cake into 48 pieces. Place cakes on wire rack over pan to catch drippings. While icing is hot, spoon or ladle icing over cakes allowing icing to coat all sides. Decorate as desired. When icing is just firm to the touch, transfer cakes to waxed paper-lined tray.

## Petit Four Icing

4  cups granulated sugar

1/4  teaspoon cream of tartar

2  cups water

3  cups powdered sugar

1/4  teaspoon almond extract or 1/2 teaspoon vanilla

*Makes 3 1/2 cups icing*

1 Stir together granulated sugar, cream of tartar and water in 2-quart heavy saucepan. Heat to a boil over medium-high heat. Cook without stirring until temperature reaches 230°F on candy thermometer.

2 Remove syrup from heat. Pour into mixing bowl. Gradually beat powdered sugar and extract into syrup mixture until icing is thick enough to coat a metal spoon. Transfer icing to microwaveable 4-cup measuring cup. Add more powdered sugar for thicker icing or stir in water, 1 teaspoon at a time, for thinner icing.

# Baklava

4 cups slivered almonds and/or walnuts (1 pound)

1¼ cups sugar, divided

2 teaspoons ground cinnamon

¼ teaspoon ground cloves

1 package (16 ounces) frozen phyllo dough (about 20 sheets), thawed

1 cup butter, melted

1½ cups water

¾ cup honey

2 (2-inch-long) strips lemon peel

1 tablespoon freshly squeezed lemon juice

1 cinnamon stick

3 whole cloves

*Makes about 32 pieces*

1 Place half the nuts in food processor. Process using on/off pulsing action until nuts are finely chopped, but not pasty. Remove from container. Repeat with remaining nuts.

2 Combine nuts, ½ cup sugar, cinnamon and cloves in medium bowl; mix well.

3 Unroll phyllo dough and place on large sheet of waxed paper. Cut phyllo sheets in half crosswise to form 2 stacks, each about 13×9 inches. Cover phyllo with plastic wrap and damp, clean kitchen towel.

4 Preheat oven to 325°F. Brush 13×9-inch baking dish with melted butter. Place 1 phyllo sheet in bottom of dish, folding in edges if too long; brush surface with butter. Repeat with 7 more phyllo sheets, brushing surface of each sheet with butter as they are layered. Sprinkle about ½ cup nut mixture evenly over layered phyllo.

5 Top nuts with 3 more layers of phyllo, brushing each sheet with butter. Sprinkle another ½ cup nut mixture on top. Repeat layering and brushing of 3 phyllo sheets with ½ cup nut mixture until there are a total of 8 (3-sheet) layers. Top final layer of nut mixture with remaining 8 phyllo sheets, brushing each sheet with butter.

6 Cut Baklava lengthwise into 4 equal sections, and then cut diagonally at 1½-inch intervals to form diamond shapes. Sprinkle top lightly with water to prevent top phyllo layers from curling up during baking. Bake 50 to 60 minutes or until golden brown.

7 To prepare syrup, combine 1½ cups water, remaining ¾ cup sugar, honey, lemon peel, lemon juice, cinnamon stick and whole cloves in medium saucepan. Bring to a boil over high heat. Reduce heat to low; simmer 15 minutes. Strain hot syrup; drizzle evenly over hot Baklava. Cool completely before serving.

Persian Roast Chicken with Walnut-Pomegranate Sauce
*(recipe on page 146)*

# entrées

As the grand centerpiece of a meal, the entrée
attracts the most attention. So why not make it
elegant and memorable?

These recipes bring entrées from garden-variety
to gourmet with dishes such as Orange-Glazed
Salmon and Persian Roast Chicken. Read on,
and tap into your inner chef as you break into new
frontiers of flavor or elaborate on the familiar.

# Persian Roast Chicken with Walnut-Pomegranate Sauce

*(photo on page 144)*

- 1 tablespoon ground cumin
- 1 tablespoon freshly squeezed lemon juice
- 2 teaspoons grated fresh lemon peel
- 1 teaspoon turmeric
- $1/4$ teaspoon saffron threads, lightly crushed
- $1/8$ teaspoon ground cinnamon
- 1 teaspoon salt
- $1/4$ teaspoon black pepper
- 1 ($4^{1}/_{2}$- to 5-pound) chicken, cut into 8 pieces
- 2 tablespoons olive oil
- Walnut-Pomegranate Sauce (recipe follows)
- Fresh pomegranate kernels (optional)

*Makes 4 servings*

1 Preheat oven to 375°F. Coat shallow roasting pan with nonstick cooking spray.

2 Combine cumin, lemon juice, lemon peel, turmeric, saffron, cinnamon, salt and pepper in bowl; mix well to form paste. Rub mixture over chicken to lightly coat. Heat oil in large skillet over medium-high heat. Add chicken, in batches if necessary, and cook until lightly browned, about 4 minutes per side. Transfer to prepared baking sheet and roast until thermometer inserted into thickest part of each piece registers 170°F, about 25 to 28 minutes.

3 Divide chicken among 4 plates. Top with walnut sauce and garnish with pomegranate kernels.

## Walnut-Pomegranate Sauce

- 2 cups thinly sliced onion
- 2 cups unsweetened pomegranate juice
- $1/2$ cup sugar
- $1/2$ teaspoon ground cumin
- $1/8$ teaspoon saffron threads, lightly crushed
- $1/4$ cup finely chopped walnuts
- $1/4$ teaspoon salt
- $1/4$ teaspoon black pepper

Place skillet over medium-high heat and add onions. Cook, stirring often, until light golden, about 8 to 10 minutes. Stir in pomegranate juice, sugar, cumin and saffron. Bring to a boil and cook, stirring occasionally, until mixture is syrupy and reduced by about half, 10 to 11 minutes. Remove from heat and stir in walnuts, salt and pepper.

# Scallops Provençal

1 tablespoon butter

1 tablespoon olive oil

4 cloves garlic, minced

1 pound bay or sea scallops

¼ pound fresh mushrooms, sliced ¼ inch thick

1 can (28 ounces) Italian tomatoes, seeded, coarsely chopped, juice reserved

2 tablespoons red wine

2 tablespoons chopped fresh parsley

1 tablespoon lemon juice

¼ teaspoon dried oregano

¼ teaspoon dried basil

Salt black pepper

Hot cooked rice

---

**TIP**

*When selecting scallops, choose those that are translucent and shiny in appearance and have a sweet aroma.*

*Makes 4 servings*

1 Heat butter and olive oil in 12-inch skillet over medium heat. Add garlic and cook and stir 1 minute. Add scallops and cook and stir 1 minute. Add mushrooms and cook 1 minute more.

2 Add tomatoes and their juice, red wine, parsley, lemon juice and oregano; stir well. Reduce heat and simmer 5 to 7 minutes. Taste and season with basil, salt and pepper. Serve immediately with hot cooked rice.

# Smoked Turkey Breast
## with Chipotle Rub

Mesquite or hickory wood chips

2 tablespoons packed dark brown sugar

2 tablespoons ground cumin

1 tablespoon garlic powder

1 tablespoon smoked paprika

1 tablespoon salt

2 teaspoons ground chipotle pepper

1 teaspoon chili powder

4 tablespoons unsalted butter, softened

1 (5¹/₂- to 6-pound) bone-in, skin-on turkey breast, rinsed and patted dry

*Makes 8 to 10 servings*

1 Prepare grill for medium-hot indirect cooking, about 325°F to 350°F. Place wood chips in bowl of water; let soak at least 30 minutes.

2 Combine sugar, cumin, garlic powder, paprika, salt, chipotle pepper and chili powder in bowl; mix well. Place 2 tablespoons mixture in separate bowl; mix with butter until combined.

3 Using your finger, gently loosen skin over breast. Spread butter mixture under skin directly onto breast meat. Rub skin and cavity of turkey with remaining spice mixture.

4 Remove some wood chips from water; place in small aluminum tray or one made using foil. Place tray under grill rack directly on heat source. Allow wood to begin to smolder, about 10 minutes. Place turkey onto grill grid away from heat source; close lid and cook 1 hour.

5 Replenish wood chips after 1 hour. Grill turkey until thermometer inserted into thickest portion registers 170°F. Transfer to cutting board; let stand about 10 minutes before slicing.

# Grilled Strip Steaks
## with Fresh Chimichurri

4 (8-ounce) bone-in strip
   steaks (about 1 inch thick)

³/₄ teaspoon ground cumin

³/₄ teaspoon salt

¹/₄ teaspoon black pepper
   Chimichurri (recipe follows)

*Makes 4 servings*

**1** Prepare grill for direct heat cooking and heat to hot. Sprinkle both sides of each steak with cumin, salt and pepper. Place on oiled grill grid over heat source.

**2** Grill steaks, turning once, 4 to 5 minutes per side for medium-rare, 5 to 7 minutes for medium. Divide steaks among 4 serving plates; serve with Chimichurri.

## Chimichurri

¹/₂ cup packed fresh basil leaves

¹/₄ cup packed fresh parsley

¹/₃ cup extra-virgin olive oil

 2 tablespoons packed fresh cilantro leaves

 1 clove garlic

 2 tablespoons lemon juice

¹/₄ teaspoon ground coriander

¹/₂ teaspoon grated orange peel

¹/₂ teaspoon salt

¹/₈ teaspoon black pepper

Combine all ingredients in blender. Purée, shaking blender occasionally if needed.

# Pork Chops with Sweet Potatoes and Apples

4 slices bacon

4 pork loin chops (1 inch thick), fat trimmed

1 tablespoon lemon juice

3 medium sweet potatoes, peeled and shredded

3 medium apples, peeled, cored and shredded

1 small onion, shredded

1/4 teaspoon salt

1/8 teaspoon black pepper

1/8 teaspoon ground nutmeg

1/4 teaspoon dried chervil

1 tablespoon chopped fresh parsley

*Makes 4 servings*

1 Cook bacon in 12-inch skillet over medium-high heat until crisp. Drain all but 1 tablespoon fat. Crumble bacon and set aside.

2 Rub pork chops with lemon juice; brown in bacon fat. Remove from pan and set aside. Drain all but 1 tablespoon fat. Add sweet potatoes, apples and onion to pan. Cook 5 minutes, stirring occasionally. Add salt, pepper, nutmeg and chervil; mix well.

3 Place vegetable mixture in greased 9×9×2-inch pan. Arrange pork chops on top of mixture; sprinkle with chopped parsley and bacon. Cover tightly and bake at 350°F for 50 to 60 minutes or until pork chops are tender. Serve immediately.

# Roasted Pork Tenderloin
## with Fresh Plum Salsa

2 to 3 limes

Fresh Plum Salsa (recipe follows)

1 well-trimmed whole pork tenderloin (about 1 pound)

⅓ cup soy sauce

1 tablespoon dark sesame oil

2 cloves garlic, minced

2 tablespoons packed brown sugar

Fresh cilantro sprigs (optional)

Lime wedges (optional)

*Makes 4 servings*

1 Cut limes crosswise in half; squeeze with citrus reamer to extract juice into measuring cup. Measure 2 tablespoons; set aside. Prepare Fresh Plum Salsa using remaining juice.

2 Place tenderloin in large resealable food storage bag. Combine soy sauce, 2 tablespoons lime juice, oil and garlic in small bowl. Pour over tenderloin. Seal bag tightly, turning to coat. Marinate in refrigerator overnight, turning occasionally.

3 Preheat oven to 375°F. Drain tenderloin, reserving 2 tablespoons marinade. Combine reserved marinade and sugar in small saucepan. Bring to a boil over medium-high heat. Cook 1 minute, stirring once; set aside.

4 To ensure even cooking, tuck narrow end of tenderloin under roast forming even thickness. Secure with butcher's string. Place tenderloin on meat rack in shallow roasting pan. Brush with reserved sugar mixture.

5 Insert meat thermometer into tenderloin. Bake 15 minutes; brush with remaining sugar mixture. Bake 10 minutes more or until thermometer registers 160°F.

6 Transfer tenderloin to cutting board; tent with foil. Let stand 10 minutes. Remove string from tenderloin; discard. Carve tenderloin into thin slices with carving knife. Serve with Fresh Plum Salsa. Garnish with cilantro and lime wedges.

## Fresh Plum Salsa

*Makes 1 cup*

2 cups coarsely chopped red plums (about 3)

2 tablespoons chopped green onion

2 tablespoons packed brown sugar

1 tablespoon chopped fresh cilantro

2 teaspoons freshly squeezed lime juice

Dash ground red pepper

Combine all ingredients in small bowl. Cover; refrigerate at least 2 hours.

# Mustard Crusted **Rib Roast**

1   (3-rib) beef rib roast, trimmed* (6 to 7 pounds)

3   tablespoons Dijon mustard

1   tablespoon plus 1½ teaspoons chopped fresh tarragon or 1½ teaspoons dried tarragon

3   cloves garlic, minced

¼   cup dry red wine

⅓   cup finely chopped shallots (about 2 shallots)

1   tablespoon all-purpose flour

1   cup beef broth

Mashed potatoes (optional)

*Ask your butcher to remove the chine bone (or back bone) for easier carving. Trim fat to ¼-inch thickness.

*Makes 6 to 8 servings*

1. Preheat oven to 450°F. Place roast, bone-side down, in shallow roasting pan. Combine mustard, tarragon and garlic in small bowl; spread over all surfaces of roast except bottom. Insert meat thermometer into thickest part of roast, not touching bone or fat. Roast 10 minutes.

2. Reduce oven temperature to 350°F. Roast 2½ to 3 hours for medium or until internal temperature reaches 145°F when tested with meat thermometer inserted into thickest part of roast, not touching bone.

3. Transfer roast to cutting board; cover with foil. Let stand 10 to 15 minutes before carving. Internal temperature will continue to rise 5°F to 10°F during stand time.

4. To make gravy, pour drippings from roasting pan, reserving 1 tablespoon in medium saucepan. Add wine to roasting pan; place over 2 burners. Cook over medium heat 2 minutes or until slightly thickened, stirring to scrape up browned bits; set aside.

5. Add shallots to reserved drippings in saucepan; cook and stir over medium heat 4 minutes or until softened. Add flour; cook and stir 1 minute. Add broth and wine mixture; cook 5 minutes or until sauce thickens, stirring occasionally. Pour through strainer into gravy boat, pressing with back of spoon on shallots; discard solids.

6. Carve roast into ½-inch-thick slices. Serve with gravy and mashed potatoes, if desired.

# Gingered Beef and Snow Peas

3 tablespoons peanut oil

2 cloves garlic, minced

1 pound sirloin, thinly sliced

1 large onion, sliced

2 tablespoons sherry

1 package (6 ounces) frozen snow peas, thawed

1/4 pound mushrooms, sliced

3/4 cup beef broth

2 tablespoons cornstarch

2 tablespoons soy sauce

3/4 teaspoon salt

1/8 teaspoon black pepper

1/4 teaspoon ground ginger

Hot cooked rice

*Makes 4 to 6 servings*

1 Heat 1 tablespoon oil in 12-inch skillet or wok over medium heat. Add garlic and meat. Stir-fry 3 minutes or until meat is cooked. Remove from pan and set aside.

2 Heat remaining oil in pan. Add onion and stir-fry 1 minute. Add sherry and cook 30 seconds. Add snow peas and stir-fry 1 minute. Add mushrooms and stir-fry 1 minute more.

3 Return beef to pan. Mix beef broth, cornstarch, soy sauce, salt, pepper and ground ginger together. Add to pan and cook, stirring occasionally, until thickened. Serve immediately over hot cooked rice.

# Braised Lamb Mediterranean

¼ cup all-purpose flour

1 teaspoon salt

¼ teaspoon black pepper

3 pounds lamb chops or shanks

2 tablespoons olive oil

2 carrots, peeled and shredded

1 large onion, sliced

¼ pound fresh green beans, sliced

1 clove garlic, minced

½ cup dry white wine

½ cup water

1 can (6 ounces) tomato paste

3 tablespoons chopped fresh dill

2 tablespoons chopped fresh parsley

1 teaspoon dried oregano

*Makes 4 servings*

**1** Combine flour, salt and pepper; dredge meat in flour mixture. Heat olive oil in 12-inch skillet over medium heat. Brown meat on all sides. Remove from pan and drain excess oil. Add carrots, onion, green beans and garlic. Cook and stir 2 minutes.

**2** Place vegetables in greased 13×9×2-inch pan. Arrange meat on top. Combine white wine, water, tomato paste, dill, parsley and oregano. Pour over meat and vegetables. Cover tightly and bake at 350°F for 2 hours or until meat is tender. Serve immediately.

# Beef **Roulade**

1½  pounds ground beef
1½  cups fresh bread crumbs
  2  eggs
¾  cup milk
½  cup ketchup
¼  cup Parmesan cheese
¼  cup chopped fresh parsley
1½  teaspoons dried oregano
⅛  teaspoon garlic powder
½  teaspoon salt
¼  teaspoon black pepper
  2  packages (10 ounces each)
      frozen chopped spinach,
      thawed
  1  cup ricotta cheese

*Makes 14 (1-inch) servings*

1 Place ground beef, bread crumbs, eggs, milk, ketchup, Parmesan cheese, parsley, oregano, garlic powder, salt and pepper in large bowl. Mix thoroughly, but gently, with hands until well combined. Turn out onto waxed paper and shape into 10×14-inch rectangle.

2 Place spinach in towel and wring until very dry. Place spinach and ricotta cheese in bowl of electric stand mixer. Turn to low and mix 1 minute. Spread spinach mixture on top of meat mixture. Roll up, beginning at longest side. Press edges and ends of roll together to seal.

3 Place on greased baking sheet, seam-side down. Bake at 350°F for 1 hour. Serve immediately.

# Chicken Piccata

3 tablespoons all-purpose flour

$^1/_2$ teaspoon salt

$^1/_4$ teaspoon black pepper

4 boneless, skinless chicken breasts (4 ounces each)

2 teaspoons olive oil

1 teaspoon butter

2 cloves garlic, minced

$^3/_4$ cup fat-free, reduced-sodium chicken broth

1 tablespoon fresh lemon juice

2 tablespoons chopped fresh Italian parsley

1 tablespoon drained capers

*Makes 4 servings*

1 Combine flour, salt and pepper in shallow dish. Reserve 1 tablespoon flour mixture.

2 Place chicken between sheets of plastic wrap. Using flat side of meat mallet or rolling pin, pound chicken to $^1/_2$-inch thickness. Coat chicken in flour mixture, shaking off excess.

3 Heat oil and butter in large nonstick skillet over medium heat until butter is melted. Cook chicken 4 to 5 minutes per side or until no longer pink in center. Transfer to serving platter; cover loosely with foil.

4 Add garlic to same skillet; cook and stir over medium heat 1 minute. Add reserved flour mixture; cook and stir 1 minute. Add broth and lemon juice; cook 2 minutes, stirring frequently, until sauce thickens. Stir in parsley and capers; spoon sauce over chicken.

# Cornish Hens
## with Wild Rice Stuffing

2 tablespoons butter

2 stalks celery, cut into
   ½-inch pieces

¾ cup dried apricots

2 cups cooked wild and white
   rice

½ teaspoon salt

⅛ teaspoon ground allspice

4 Cornish game hens

8 slices bacon

*Makes 4 servings*

1 Heat butter in skillet over medium heat. Add celery and cook and stir 2 minutes. Remove celery from pan; set aside.

2 Place celery and apricots in bowl of food processor; pulse until coarsely ground. Add butter from skillet, rice, salt and allspice; mix well.

3 Stuff each hen with mixture. Truss hens and crisscross 2 strips bacon over each hen. Place on rack in baking pan and bake at 350°F for 1½ to 2 hours. Serve immediately.

# Mu Shu **Pork**

½ pound boneless pork loin,
   thinly sliced

1 tablespoon sherry

1 tablespoon soy sauce

1 teaspoon cornstarch

½ teaspoon sugar

¼ teaspoon ground ginger

4 teaspoons vegetable oil

3 eggs, beaten

¼ head cabbage, sliced

1 stalk celery, sliced

½ cup chopped green onions

1 teaspoon sesame seeds

*Makes 4 servings*

1 Combine pork, sherry, soy sauce, cornstarch, sugar and ground ginger in medium bowl; mix well and set aside.

2 Heat 2 teaspoons oil in 12-inch skillet or wok over medium heat. Add eggs and scramble until very dry; break into small pieces. Remove from pan and set aside.

3 Heat remaining oil in pan and add pork mixture. Stir-fry until pork is thoroughly cooked. Add cabbage and celery to pan and stir-fry 2 minutes. Add eggs, green onions and sesame seeds. Stir-fry 1 minute. Serve immediately.

| entrées

# Orange-Glazed Salmon

## Glaze

- 2 tablespoons orange juice
- 2 tablespoons soy sauce
- 1 tablespoon honey
- 3/4 teaspoon grated fresh ginger
- 1/2 teaspoon rice wine vinegar
- 1/4 teaspoon sesame oil

## Salmon

- 4 salmon fillets (about 6 ounces each)
- 1/2 teaspoon salt
- 1/4 teaspoon black pepper
- 1 tablespoon olive oil

*Makes 4 servings*

1 For glaze, whisk orange juice, soy sauce, honey, ginger, vinegar and sesame oil in small bowl; set aside.

2 Season salmon with salt and pepper. Heat olive oil in medium nonstick skillet over medium-high heat. Place salmon, skin side up, in skillet; brush with glaze. Cook salmon 4 minutes or just until center is opaque. Carefully turn; brush with some remaining glaze. Cook 4 minutes or until salmon just begins to flake when tested with fork. Transfer salmon to serving plate; cover and keep warm.

3 Meanwhile, place remaining glaze in small saucepan; cook and stir until thickened and reduced to about 2 tablespoons. Serve over salmon.

# Flounder Florentine

5 tablespoons butter, divided

2 tablespoons all-purpose flour

$^1/_8$ teaspoon ground nutmeg

1 teaspoon salt

$^1/_4$ teaspoon black pepper

$^2/_3$ cup milk

1 package (10 ounces) frozen chopped spinach, thawed

1 clove garlic

1 small onion, quartered

1 tablespoon olive oil

1 tablespoon lemon juice

3 tablespoons fresh bread crumbs

4 fresh flounder filets (4 ounces each)

*Makes 4 servings*

1 Melt 2 tablespoons butter in small saucepan over medium heat. Add flour and cook 1 minute. Stir in nutmeg, salt and pepper. Gradually add milk and cook, stirring occasionally, until thickened. Remove from heat and set aside.

2 Place spinach in towel and wring until very dry. Place spinach, garlic and onion in food processor; pulse until finely chopped.

3 Heat olive oil in 12-inch skillet over medium heat. Add spinach mixture and lemon juice; cook 2 minutes. Add milk mixture and cook 1 minute more.

4 Place one-fourth of spinach mixture on each piece of flounder. Roll and secure with toothpick. Place rolls in greased 9×9×2-inch pan.

5 Sprinkle with bread crumbs and dot with remaining butter. Bake at 350°F for 30 minutes. Serve immediately.

# Moroccan-Style Lamb Chops

1 tablespoon olive oil

1 teaspoon ground cumin

1 teaspoon ground coriander

3/4 teaspoon salt

1/8 teaspoon ground cinnamon

1/8 teaspoon ground red pepper

4 center-cut lamb loin chops, cut 1 inch thick (about 1 pound total)

2 cloves garlic, minced

**HINT**

*This recipe also works well using a grill pan on top of your range.*

*Makes 4 servings*

1 Prepare grill or preheat broiler. Combine oil, cumin, coriander, salt, cinnamon and red pepper in small bowl; mix well. Rub or brush oil mixture over both sides of lamb chops. Sprinkle garlic over both sides of lamb chops.

2 Grill on covered grill or broil 4 to 5 inches from heat, 5 minutes per side for medium doneness.

# Grilled Swordfish Sicilian Style

3 tablespoons extra-virgin olive oil

1 clove garlic, minced

2 tablespoons lemon juice

$^3/_4$ teaspoon salt

$^1/_8$ teaspoon black pepper

3 tablespoons capers, drained

1 tablespoon chopped fresh oregano or basil

1$^1/_2$ pounds swordfish steaks ($^3/_4$ inch thick)

*Makes 4 to 6 servings*

1 Prepare grill for direct cooking. For sauce, heat olive oil in small saucepan over low heat; add garlic. Cook 1 minute. Remove from heat; cool slightly. Whisk in lemon juice, salt and pepper until salt is dissolved. Stir in capers and oregano.

2 Place swordfish on oiled grid over medium heat. Grill 7 to 8 minutes, turning once, or until center is opaque. Serve fish with sauce.

# Filet Mignon
## with Tarragon Butter

2 (8-ounce) trimmed beef
   tenderloin steaks
   ($1^{1}/_{4}$ to $1^{1}/_{2}$ inches thick)

2 teaspoons olive oil

$^{1}/_{4}$ teaspoon kosher salt

$^{1}/_{8}$ teaspoon black pepper

2 tablespoons butter

1 clove garlic, minced

2 teaspoons chopped fresh
   tarragon or $^{3}/_{4}$ teaspoon
   dried tarragon

*Makes 2 servings*

1 Rub steaks with olive oil. Sprinkle with salt and pepper; let stand at
room temperature 15 minutes.

2 Heat medium skillet over medium-high heat. Cook steaks about
10 minutes, turning once, to 140°F for rare or to desired doneness.
Transfer to serving plate; tent loosely with foil.

3 Melt butter in same skillet until it begins to brown slightly, scraping
up any browned bits. Add garlic; cook about 15 seconds or until
fragrant. Stir in tarragon. Pour sauce over steaks; serve immediately.

# Sea Bass with Asian Black Bean Paste

2  (1½-pound) striped bass, cleaned, heads and tails intact, rinsed and patted dry

1  tablespoon grated fresh ginger

1  bunch green onions, chopped

3  tablespoons sake

2  tablespoons reduced-sodium soy sauce

2  tablespoons black bean garlic sauce

2  teaspoons sugar

1  teaspoon Asian sesame oil

1  Preheat oven to 450°F. Lightly oil 13×11-inch roasting pan. With sharp knife, cut 3 parallel slashes, about ½-inch deep, on each side of fish; rub ginger into slashes. Sprinkle half of green onions over bottom of prepared roasting pan.

2  Combine sake, soy sauce, black bean sauce, sugar and sesame oil in small bowl. Place fish on top of onions in roasting pan and spoon half of sake mixture over fish. Turn fish over and repeat with remaining sake mixture. Sprinkle with remaining green onions; cover tightly with foil.

3  Place in center of oven and bake until fish is cooked through and flakes easily with a fork, 30 to 35 minutes. Transfer fish to serving platter; spoon liquid from pan over fish before serving.

# Herb-Roasted Racks of Lamb

1/2 cup mango chutney, chopped

2 to 3 cloves garlic, minced

2 whole racks (6 ribs each) lamb loin chops (2 1/2 to 3 pounds)

1 cup fresh bread crumbs

1 tablespoon chopped fresh thyme or 1 teaspoon dried thyme

1 tablespoon chopped fresh rosemary or 1 teaspoon dried rosemary

1 tablespoon chopped fresh oregano or 1 teaspoon dried oregano

*Makes 4 servings*

1 Preheat oven to 400°F. Combine chutney and garlic in small bowl; spread evenly over meaty side of lamb. Combine remaining ingredients in separate small bowl; pat crumb mixture evenly over chutney mixture on lamb chops.

2 Place lamb racks, crumb sides up, on rack in shallow roasting pan. Roast 30 to 35 minutes for medium or until internal temperature reaches 145°F when tested with meat thermometer inserted into thickest part of lamb, not touching bone.

3 Remove lamb to cutting board; tent with foil. Let stand 10 to 15 minutes before carving. (Internal temperature will continue to rise 5°F to 10°F during stand time.) Using large knife, slice between ribs to cut into individual chops. Serve immediately.

# Jamaican Baby Back Ribs

2  tablespoons sugar

2  tablespoons fresh lemon juice

1  tablespoon salt

1  tablespoon vegetable oil

2  teaspoons black pepper

2  teaspoons dried thyme

$3/4$  teaspoon ground cinnamon

$3/4$  teaspoon ground nutmeg

$3/4$  teaspoon ground allspice

$1/2$  teaspoon ground red pepper

6  pounds well-trimmed pork baby back ribs, cut into 3- to 4-rib portions

Barbecue Sauce (recipe follows)

*Makes 6 servings*

1 Combine all ingredients except ribs and Barbecue Sauce in small bowl; stir well. Press seasoning onto ribs. Cover; refrigerate overnight. Prepare grill for indirect cooking. Prepare Barbecue Sauce.

2 Place seasoned ribs on grid directly over drip pan over medium-low heat. Grill covered 1 hour, turning occasionally. Baste ribs generously with Barbecue Sauce; grill 30 minutes more or until ribs are tender and browned, turning occasionally.

3 Bring remaining Barbecue Sauce to a boil over medium-high heat; boil at least 1 minute. Serve ribs with heated sauce.

## Barbecue Sauce

*Makes about 2 cups*

2  tablespoons butter

$1/2$  cup finely chopped onion

$1 1/2$  cups ketchup

1  cup red currant jelly

$1/4$  cup cider vinegar

1  tablespoon soy sauce

$1/4$  teaspoon ground red pepper

$1/4$  teaspoon ground black pepper

Melt butter in medium saucepan over medium-high heat. Add onion; cook and stir until softened. Stir in remaining ingredients. Reduce heat to medium-low; simmer 20 minutes, stirring often.

# Homemade Italian **Sausage**

3 pounds pork shoulder,
   cut into 1-inch cubes*

3 teaspoons salt

1¹/₂ teaspoons black pepper

1¹/₄ teaspoons ground red pepper

2 cloves garlic, minced

1 teaspoon onion powder

1 teaspoon paprika

¹/₈ teaspoon dried marjoram

¹/₈ teaspoon dried rosemary

¹/₈ teaspoon dried thyme

¹/₂ cup dry red wine

1 tablespoon shortening
   Natural or synthetic casings,
   prepared for use per
   instructions

*You may make sausage with fresh ground
pork from your butcher or supermarket. Toss
with spices as instructed, and then skip to
step 3, stirring wine into ground pork and
continue as directed.

*Makes 3 pounds sausage*

1 Place pork on metal baking sheet and freeze 20 minutes. Combine salt, black pepper, red pepper, garlic, onion powder, paprika, marjoram, rosemary and thyme in small bowl. Sprinkle mixture over pork; toss to coat evenly.

2 Process one-third of pork at a time in food processor (return remaining pork to freezer) until coarsely ground, or run pork through meat grinder fitted with coarse grinding plate. Transfer ground pork to large bowl and place in freezer; repeat with remaining pork.

3 Remove ground pork from freezer. Pour wine over ground pork. Stir vigorously with wooden spoon until well combined.

4 Assemble and attach sausage press according to manufacturer's directions, greasing nozzle with shortening. Slide prepared casings onto nozzle tightly. Tie off end of casing with butcher's twine. Follow manufacturer's directions for stuffing sausage into casings. Twist sausage into smaller links as desired and refrigerate or freeze until ready to use.

# Traditional Greek Moussaka

3 medium eggplants, sliced
   $1/4$ inch thick

$1/2$ cup water

3 medium onions, cut into
   sixths

2 cloves garlic

2 pounds boneless lamb, cut
   into 1-inch cubes

2 tablespoons olive oil

1 can (8 ounces) tomato sauce

6 tablespoons tomato paste

1 tablespoon sugar

$1/2$ cup dry red wine

$1/2$ teaspoon ground cinnamon

$1/2$ teaspoon ground nutmeg

1 bay leaf

$1/2$ teaspoon dried basil

$1/2$ teaspoon salt

$1/4$ teaspoon black pepper

$1/2$ cup (1 stick) butter

6 tablespoons all-purpose
   flour

4 cups milk

4 eggs, beaten

$1/2$ cup bread crumbs

$1^3/_4$ cups Parmesan cheese,
   divided

*Makes 8 servings*

1 Arrange eggplant in 13×9×2-inch pan; sprinkle with water. Cover tightly and bake at 400°F for 30 minutes. Drain on paper towels; set aside.

2 Place onions, garlic and lamb in food processor and pulse until coarsely ground. Heat oil in 12-inch skillet over medium heat. Add ground lamb mixture and cook until browned; drain well. Add tomato sauce, tomato paste, sugar, red wine, cinnamon, nutmeg, bay leaf, basil, salt and pepper; mix well. Reduce heat and simmer 30 minutes. Remove bay leaf.

3 Melt butter in large saucepan over medium heat. Add flour and stir until smooth. Gradually add milk, stirring constantly; cook until mixture thickens. Add eggs, bread crumbs and $1^1/_2$ cups Parmesan cheese. Remove from heat and set aside.

4 Arrange half of eggplant slices in greased 13×19×2-inch pan. Top with meat mixture. Sprinkle remaining $1/4$ cup Parmesan cheese over meat mixture and top with remaining eggplant. Spread milk mixture over eggplant. Bake at 350°F for 50 to 60 minutes or until top is brown. Cool 15 minutes before serving.

# Black Bean Flautas
## with Charred Tomatillo Salsa

**Salsa**

- 1 jalapeño pepper*
- 1 pound tomatillos, unpeeled
- 1 small yellow onion, unpeeled
- 6 cloves garlic, unpeeled
  Juice of ½ lime
  Salt and black pepper

**Flautas**

- 1 can (15 ounces) black beans, with liquid
- 1 cup vegetable broth
- 1 teaspoon salt, divided
- ½ teaspoon ground cumin
- ½ teaspoon chili powder
- 3 cloves garlic, peeled and minced
- ¼ cup chopped fresh cilantro
  Juice of 1 lime
- 10 flour tortillas
- 2½ cups shredded Colby-Jack cheese
- 1 cup seeded and chopped tomatoes (about 2 tomatoes)
- 1 cup thinly sliced green onions

*Jalapeño peppers can sting and irritate the skin, so wear rubber gloves when handling peppers and do not touch your eyes.

*Makes 5 servings and 2 cups salsa*

1 **For salsa:** In large, heavy, dry skillet over medium-high heat, cook unpeeled jalapeño, tomatillos, onion and garlic, stirring frequently, about 20 minutes or until soft and skins are blackened. Remove from skillet; allow to cool 5 minutes. Peel tomatillos, onion and garlic, and remove stem and seeds from jalapeño; place in blender or food processor with lime juice. Blend until smooth. Season to taste with salt and pepper. Set aside.

2 **For flautas:** Place beans and liquid, vegetable broth, ½ teaspoon salt, cumin, chili powder and garlic in medium saucepan. Bring to a boil. Reduce heat; simmer 10 minutes or until beans are very soft. Drain, reserving liquid. Purée drained bean mixture with cilantro, remaining ½ teaspoon salt and lime juice in blender or food processor until smooth. (Add reserved liquid 1 teaspoon at a time if beans are dry.)

3 Preheat oven to 450°F. Spread 1 to 2 tablespoons bean purée on tortilla; sprinkle with about ¼ cup cheese, 2 tablespoons tomatoes and 1½ tablespoons green onions. Roll up very tightly and place seam side down in 13×9-inch baking dish. Repeat with remaining tortillas, rolling tightly to fit flautas into dish. (You should be able to fit 8 flautas across and 2 more on side of dish lengthwise.) Bake 10 to 15 minutes or until crisp and brown and cheese is melted. Serve with salsa.

Five Mushroom Risotto
*(recipe on page 176)*

# pasta, rice, and grains

Nearly every world cuisine uses pastas and grains as a staple, and each cuisine lends unique preparations and flavors to the same basic ingredients; the same pasta can be used to create a classic spaghetti or a bowl of Asian noodle soup.

These simple dinnertime staples become an art form as we show you how to make your own noodles, add elegant twists to classic dishes, and explore the possibilities of cooking with lesser-known grains.

# Five Mushroom **Risotto**

*(photo on page 174)*

2 tablespoons olive oil, divided

3 tablespoons butter, divided

1 shallot, minced

¼ cup minced fresh parsley

¼ cup white wine

½ cup each fresh shiitake, chanterelle, portobello, oyster and white mushrooms, wiped clean of dirt and chopped into ½-inch pieces

½ teaspoon coarse salt

1 cup arborio rice

4 cups (1 quart) chicken or vegetable broth, heated to just under a boil

¼ cup grated Parmesan cheese

½ cup cream

Salt and black pepper to taste

White truffle oil (optional)

*Makes 4 servings*

1 Heat 1 tablespoon olive oil in deep saucepan over medium-high heat; add 2 tablespoons butter. When butter has melted, add shallot and cook and stir 30 to 45 seconds or until shallot is just beginning to brown. Add parsley and mix well, cooking 30 seconds more.

2 Add wine and stir constantly until wine evaporates. Add mushrooms and mix well. Add coarse salt. When mushrooms soften and reduce their volume by half, remove from heat. Pour into bowl and set aside.

3 Add remaining olive oil to saucepan and heat 30 seconds. Add arborio rice and toss until rice is completely coated with olive oil/butter mixture. Cook 1 to 2 minutes or until edges of rice become translucent.

4 Reduce heat to medium-low and add ½ cup of hot broth, mixing constantly with a wooden spoon until rice absorbs broth.

5 Add another ½ cup broth and mix constantly until absorbed. Repeat. When only ½ cup broth remains, add mushroom mixture to risotto. Mix well; add remaining broth. Mix until absorbed. Rice will be slightly softer than al dente and creamy.

6 Add Parmesan cheese and cream, mixing well until cheese is melted and absorbed. Add salt and pepper to taste.

7 Remove from heat and stir in remaining butter. Risotto should be creamy but not watery. Serve hot garnished with truffle oil.

# Hot and Tangy Asian Noodles

 ¹/₂ cup peanut oil

 2 tablespoons rice vinegar
 or white wine vinegar

 1 tablespoon dry sherry

2¹/₂ tablespoons sesame oil

 3 tablespoons soy sauce

 1 tablespoon red pepper flakes

 ¹/₂ teaspoon ground ginger

 1 tablespoon packed brown
 sugar

 1 tablespoon chopped onion

 ¹/₄ cup diced green pepper

 1 recipe Basic Egg Noodle
 Pasta or 1¹/₂ pounds
 spaghetti, cooked and
 drained

### TIP

*To cook pasta, add 1 tablespoon salt and 1 tablespoon oil to 6 quarts boiling water. Gradually add pasta and continue to cook at a slow boil until pasta is "al dente" or slightly firm to the bite. Pasta floats on top of the water as it cooks, so stir occasionally to keep pasta cooking evenly. When done cooking, drain in a colander.*

*Makes 8 servings*

Combine all ingredients. Toss well and refrigerate 2 hours, stirring occasionally.

## Basic Egg Noodle Pasta

*Makes 1¹/₄ pounds dough*

 4 large eggs (⁷/₈ cup eggs)

 1 tablespoon water

3¹/₂ cups sifted all-purpose flour

Place eggs, water and flour in bowl of electric stand mixer. Turn mixer to low and mix 30 seconds. Attach dough hook. Turn to low and knead 2 minutes.

Hand knead dough 30 seconds to 1 minute. Cover with dry towel and let rest 15 minutes before extruding through pasta maker.

# Couscous with Carrots and Cranberries

2 teaspoons olive oil

$^1/_2$ small onion, thinly sliced

$^1/_2$ large carrot, grated using large holes of box grater

$^1/_4$ cup chopped dried cranberries

$^1/_4$ teaspoon ground cinnamon

$^1/_4$ teaspoon ground cumin

$^1/_4$ teaspoon turmeric

1 cup whole wheat couscous

2 cups chicken or vegetable broth, heated to just under a boil

Salt

Black pepper

*Makes 4 servings*

1 Heat oil in medium skillet over medium-high heat; add onion. Cook, stirring frequently, 1 minute or until translucent. Add carrots and cook 1 minute more. Add cranberries and cook 30 seconds.

2 Add cinnamon, cumin and turmeric; mix well. Cook 15 to 20 seconds or until spices begin to release their aromas. Add couscous and mix well. Remove from heat and pour mixture into heatproof bowl.

3 Pour broth over couscous mixture. Add salt and pepper to taste and mix well. Cover tightly with plastic wrap and set aside to steam for 10 to 15 minutes. Remove plastic wrap and fluff couscous.

# Spinach Pasta Pomodoro

5 large tomatoes, cut into sixths

3 tablespoons olive oil

3 cloves garlic, minced

1/2 cup chopped fresh basil

1 teaspoon sugar

1 teaspoon salt

1/4 teaspoon black pepper

1 recipe Spinach Pasta or 1 1/2 pounds flat spinach noodles, cooked and drained

Parmesan cheese

*Makes 3 cups*

1 Run tomatoes through food mill. Measure out 3 cups purée and set aside.

2 Heat oil in 2-quart saucepan over medium heat. Add garlic and cook and stir 2 minutes. Add tomato purée, basil, sugar, salt and pepper. Reduce heat; cover and simmer 30 minutes. Serve immediately over hot pasta with Parmesan cheese.

## Spinach Pasta

*Makes 1 1/2 pounds dough*

1 package (10 ounces) frozen, chopped spinach, thawed

1 tablespoon water

4 large eggs (7/8 cup)

4 cups sifted all-purpose flour

1 Place spinach in towel and wring out all water until spinach feels very dry. Place spinach in food processor and pulse until coarsely ground. Discard unground spinach that remains in processor bowl.

2 Place ground spinach, water and eggs in bowl of electric stand mixer. Turn to medium-low and mix 30 seconds. Add flour to bowl. Turn to low and mix 45 seconds. Attach dough hook to mixer. Turn to low and knead 1 minute.

3 Hand knead dough 30 seconds to 1 minute. Cover with dry towel and let rest 15 minutes before extruding through pasta maker.

# Pasta with Creamy Vodka Sauce

6   ounces uncooked campanelle or bowtie pasta

1   tablespoon unsalted butter

3   plum tomatoes, seeded and chopped

2   cloves garlic, minced

3   tablespoons vodka

1/2   cup whipping cream

1/4   teaspoon salt

1/4   teaspoon red pepper flakes

1/3   cup grated Parmesan cheese

2   tablespoons snipped chives

*Makes 4 to 5 servings*

1 Cook pasta according to package directions; drain and return to pan. Melt butter in large skillet over medium heat. Add tomatoes and garlic; cook 3 minutes, stirring frequently. Add vodka; simmer 2 minutes or until most liquid has evaporated.

2 Stir in cream, salt and red pepper flakes; return to a simmer. Simmer 2 to 3 minutes or until slightly thickened. Remove from heat; let stand 2 minutes. Stir in cheese until melted.

3 Add sauce and chives to pasta; toss until pasta is coated. Serve immediately.

# Pesto Lasagna

1 package (16 ounces) uncooked lasagna noodles

3 tablespoons olive oil

1½ cups chopped onions

3 cloves garlic, finely chopped

3 packages (10 ounces each) frozen chopped spinach, thawed and squeezed dry

Salt and black pepper

3 cups (24 ounces) ricotta cheese

1½ cups Pesto Sauce (see recipe on page 195)

¾ cup grated Parmesan cheese

½ cup pine nuts, toasted

6 cups (16 ounces) shredded mozzarella cheese

Strips of roasted red pepper (optional)

*Makes 8 servings*

1 Preheat oven to 350°F. Spray 13×9-inch casserole or lasagna dish with nonstick cooking spray. Partially cook lasagna noodles according to package directions.

2 Heat oil in large skillet over medium-high heat. Cook and stir onions and garlic until translucent. Add spinach; cook and stir about 5 minutes. Season with salt and pepper. Transfer to large bowl.

3 Add ricotta cheese, pesto, Parmesan cheese and pine nuts to spinach mixture; mix well.

4 Layer 5 lasagna noodles, slightly overlapping, in prepared casserole. Top with one-third of ricotta mixture and one-third of mozzarella. Repeat layers twice.

5 Bake about 35 minutes or until hot and bubbly. Garnish with red bell pepper strips.

# Bolognese Sauce

2 tablespoons olive oil

2 carrots, peeled and cut into 1-inch pieces

2 stalks celery, cut into 1-inch pieces

1 large onion, cut into eighths

$^1/_4$ cup fresh parsley sprigs

$1^1/_2$ pounds ground beef

$^1/_2$ pound ground pork

3 cloves garlic

6 large ripe tomatoes, cut into sixths

1 teaspoon dried basil

1 teaspoon dried oregano

1 bay leaf

$1^1/_2$ teaspoons salt

$^1/_4$ teaspoon black pepper

2 cans (6 ounces each) tomato paste

$^1/_4$ cup water

$^1/_4$ cup dry red wine

*Makes 2 quarts*

1 Heat oil in 12-inch skillet over medium heat. Add carrots, celery, onion, parsley, ground beef, ground pork and garlic. Cook and stir 20 minutes. Remove mixture from heat and cool 10 minutes.

2 Pulse meat mixture in food processor until coarsely ground. Place mixture in 6-quart pot.

3 Run tomatoes through food mill. Measure out 4 cups purée. Add tomato purée, basil, oregano, bay leaf, salt, pepper, tomato paste, water and wine to meat mixture. Cover and simmer on medium-low heat 1 hour.

# Rice Noodles with Broccoli and Tofu

1 package (14 ounces) firm or extra-firm tofu

1 package (8 to 10 ounces) wide rice noodles

2 tablespoons peanut oil

3 medium shallots, sliced

6 cloves garlic, minced

1 jalapeño pepper,* minced

2 teaspoons minced fresh ginger

3 cups broccoli florets

3 tablespoons regular soy sauce

1 tablespoon sweet soy sauce (or substitute regular)

1 to 2 tablespoons fish sauce
   Fresh basil leaves (optional)

*Jalapeño peppers can sting and irritate the skin, so wear rubber gloves when handling peppers and do not touch your eyes.

*Makes 4 to 6 servings*

1 Slice tofu horizontally into 2 pieces, each about 1 inch thick. Place tofu on cutting board between layers of paper towels; put another cutting board on top to add weight to press moisture out of tofu. Soak rice noodles in large bowl filled with warm water; let stand 30 minutes or until soft.

2 Meanwhile, heat oil in large skillet or wok. Cut tofu into bite-size squares and blot dry. Stir-fry about 5 minutes or until tofu is speckled and light brown on all sides. Remove and reserve.

3 Add shallots, garlic, jalapeño and ginger to skillet. Stir-fry over medium-high heat 2 to 3 minutes; add broccoli and stir-fry. Cover pan; cook 3 minutes or until broccoli is crisp-tender.

4 Drain noodles well; add to skillet and stir to combine. Return tofu to skillet; add soy sauces and fish sauce. Stir-fry about 8 minutes or until noodles are coated and flavors are blended. Adjust seasoning. Garnish with basil.

# Pasta con Salsice

1½ pounds boneless pork shoulder, cut into 1-inch strips

3 cloves garlic, minced and divided

1½ tablespoons chopped fresh parsley

¾ tablespoon red pepper flakes

1 tablespoon fennel seed

2 teaspoons salt, divided

½ cup dry red wine, divided

1 tablespoon shortening

Natural or synthetic sausage casings

3 tablespoons olive oil

3 medium green peppers, seeded and sliced

3 medium onions, sliced

2 tablespoons chopped fresh basil

1½ pounds spaghetti, cooked and drained

*Makes 6 servings*

1 Grind pork and 2 cloves garlic in food processor. Add parsley, red pepper, fennel seed, 1½ teaspoons salt and ¼ cup wine; pulse until coarsely ground.

2 Place mixture in bowl of electric stand mixture. Assemble and attach sausage stuffer according to manufacturer's directions. Grease stuffer with shortening and slide casing on tightly. Tie off end of casing. Turn mixer to medium-low and stuff pork mixture into casings. Twist sausage into 12 links and set aside.

3 Heat 1 tablespoon oil in 12-inch skillet over medium heat. Add green pepper, onion and remaining garlic; cook, stirring frequently, 5 minutes. Add remaining salt, wine, olive oil and basil. Cook, stirring frequently, 3 minutes. Remove from pan and set aside.

4 Add sausages to pan and cook until done; drain fat. Add pepper and onion mixture to cooked sausages and stir gently. Serve immediately over hot pasta.

Note: Omit red pepper flakes to make mild sausage.

# Creamy Shrimp Sauce

2/3 cup olive oil

2/3 cup diced onion

4 cloves garlic, minced

2 tablespoons all-purpose flour

1 teaspoon salt

1/4 teaspoon black pepper

6 tablespoons tomato paste

1 cup dry white wine

1/2 pound cooked, shelled shrimp

1/4 cup chopped fresh parsley

2 cups heavy cream

*Makes 3 1/2 cups*

1 Heat olive oil in 12-inch skillet over medium heat. Add onion and garlic and cook, stirring, 3 minutes. Add flour, salt and pepper and cook an additional minute, stirring continuously.

2 Add tomato paste and wine. Cook 10 minutes, stirring occasionally. Add shrimp and parsley and cook an additional 3 minutes. Stir cream into shrimp mixture. Heat through, but do not boil. Serve immediately.

# Barley and Vegetable Risotto

4½ cups fat-free, reduced-
    sodium vegetable or
    chicken broth

2 teaspoons olive oil

1 small onion, diced

8 ounces sliced mushrooms

¾ cup uncooked pearl barley

1 large red bell pepper, diced

2 cups packed baby spinach

¼ cup grated Parmesan cheese

¼ teaspoon black pepper

### NOTE

*You may use your favorite
mushrooms, such as button,
cremini or shiitake, or a
combination of two or more.*

*Makes 6 (½-cup) side-dish servings*

1 Bring broth to a boil in medium saucepan. Reduce heat to low to keep broth hot.

2 Meanwhile, heat oil in large saucepan over medium heat. Add onion; cook and stir 4 minutes. Increase heat to medium-high. Add mushrooms; cook 5 minutes, stirring frequently, or until mushrooms begin to brown and liquid evaporates.

3 Add barley; cook 1 minute. Add ¼ cup broth; cook and stir about 2 minutes or until broth is almost all absorbed. Add broth, ¼ cup at a time, stirring constantly until broth is almost absorbed before adding the next. After 20 minutes of cooking, stir in bell pepper. Continue adding broth, ¼ cup at a time, until barley is tender (about 30 minutes total). Stir in spinach; cook and stir 1 minute or just until spinach is wilted. Stir in cheese and black pepper.

# Noodles with White Clam Sauce

3 cans (6½ ounces each) minced clams

½ cup (1 stick) butter

½ cup olive oil

4 cloves garlic, minced

½ cup finely chopped fresh parsley

¾ teaspoon black pepper

1 tablespoon all-purpose flour

¾ cup grated Parmesan cheese

1½ pounds spaghetti or flat noodles, cooked and drained

*Makes 6 to 8 servings*

1 Drain juice from clams into measuring cup. Allow juice to sit about 15 minutes or until sediment settles. Pour off top liquid until ¾ cup of bottom clam sediment remains. Set aside.

2 Melt butter in large skillet over medium heat. Add olive oil, garlic and parsley. Cook 3 minutes. Add minced clams and cook an additional 5 minutes. Add pepper and flour to skillet and cook 2 minutes longer, stirring constantly. Add reserved clam sediment and bring to a slow boil. Cook 1 minute.

3 Place half of noodles in serving bowl. Add 1 cup clam sauce and half of Parmesan cheese and toss. Add remaining noodles, clam sauce and Parmesan cheese. Toss again and serve immediately.

# Whole Wheat Pasta

4  large eggs (⁷/₈ cup eggs)

2  tablespoons water

3¹/₂  cups sifted whole wheat
     flour

**TIP**

*Whole wheat pasta has more fiber
than regular pasta, thus it is a
delicious and healthy alternative.*

*Makes 1¹/₄ pounds dough*

1  Place eggs, water and flour in bowl of electric stand mixer. Turn mixer
   to low and mix 30 seconds.

2  Attach dough hook to mixer. Turn mixer to low and knead 1
   minute.

3  Hand knead dough 30 seconds to 1 minute. Cover with dry towel and
   let rest 15 minutes before extruding through pasta maker.

Note: High humidity can cause pasta dough to become sticky and
difficult to extrude. To avoid this problem, prepare dough using only the
sifted flour and eggs. Stop and check consistency. If dough is too dry,
add the water, 1 teaspoon at a time, and remix using flat beater;
or knead dough with wet hands.

# Pesto Sauce

2 cups fresh basil leaves

1 cup fresh parsley sprigs

8 cloves garlic

1 teaspoon salt

$^1/_2$ teaspoon black pepper

1 cup Parmesan cheese

$^2/_3$ cup olive oil

**TIP**

*If Pesto Sauce is not used at once, place it in a jar and cover with a thin layer of olive oil to keep it from darkening. Refrigerate for up to a week or freeze for longer storage.*

*Makes 2 cups*

Place basil leaves, parsley sprigs and garlic in food processor. Add salt, pepper and Parmesan cheese. Blend 1 minute. Stop and scrape bowl. Turn processor to medium-high. Gradually add olive oil in thin, steady stream, mixing until incorporated. Use about 2 tablespoons Pesto Sauce per serving of pasta.

Deep Dish Blueberry Pie *(recipe on page 198)*

# pies
## and tarts

As the seasons change, so do the dishes that make their way to the dinner table. Nothing reflects these ever-changing flavors quite like the pies and tarts we enjoy throughout the year.

Here you will find fruit pies and tarts that incorporate the abundance of fresh produce in the summer, sweet potato and pecan pies symbolic of the holidays, and other classics that are popular all year long.

# Deep Dish Blueberry Pie

*(photo on page 196)*

6 cups fresh blueberries
   or 2 (16-ounce) packages
   frozen blueberries, thawed

2 tablespoons lemon juice

1¼ cups sugar

3 tablespoons quick tapioca

¼ teaspoon ground cinnamon
   Pie Dough for a 2-Crust Pie
   (recipe follows)

1 tablespoon butter, cut into
   4 pieces

*Makes 9 servings*

1 Preheat oven to 400°F. Place blueberries in large bowl and sprinkle with lemon juice. Stir sugar, tapioca and cinnamon together in small bowl. Gently stir sugar mixture into blueberries until blended.

2 Roll out one-half recipe of pie dough into 12-inch circle on lightly floured work surface. Fit dough into 9×2-inch deep-dish pie pan. Trim all but ½ inch of overhang. Pour blueberry mixture into pan; dot top with butter pieces.

3 Roll remaining one-half recipe of pie dough into 10-inch circle, about ¼ inch thick. Using small cookie cutter or knife, cut 4 or 5 shapes from dough for vents. Lift and center dough over blueberry mixture in pie pan. Trim dough leaving 1-inch border around pie. Fold excess dough under and even with pan edge. Press dough onto edge of pan with tines of fork.

4 Place pie in oven and bake 15 minutes at 400°F. Reduce heat to 350°F and bake an additional 40 minutes or until pastry is browned. Cool on rack about 30 minutes before serving.

## Pie Dough for a 2-Crust Pie

2½ cups all purpose flour

1 teaspoon salt

1 teaspoon sugar

1 cup (2 sticks) unsalted butter, each stick
   cut into 8 pieces and chilled

⅓ cup ice water

In large mixing bowl, stir together flour, salt and sugar. Using pastry blender, incorporate butter into flour mixture. (Mixture will resemble coarse meal with small pieces of butter still visible when thoroughly blended.)

Drizzle 2 tablespoons ice water over mixture; stir to blend. Repeat with remaining ice water. Squeeze dough together with hands and turn out onto work surface. Knead dough briefly, about 4 to 5 turns, until it just comes together. Divide dough in half and shape each half into disc. Wrap each disc in plastic wrap and refrigerate at least 1 hour before using. (Dough may be refrigerated up to 2 days or frozen up to 1 month before using. If frozen, thaw in refrigerator before using.)

**pies and tarts**

# Rustic Plum Tart

¼ cup (½ stick) plus
  1 tablespoon butter,
  divided

3 cups plum wedges (about
  6 plums)

¼ cup granulated sugar

½ cup all-purpose flour

½ cup old-fashioned or quick
  oats

¼ cup packed brown sugar

½ teaspoon ground cinnamon

¼ teaspoon salt

1 egg

1 teaspoon water

1 refrigerated pie crust (half
  of 15-ounce package)

1 tablespoon chopped
  crystallized ginger

---

**TIP**

*Use dark reddish-purple plums
and cut the fruit into 8 wedges.*

---

*Makes 1 (9-inch) tart*

1 Preheat oven to 425°F. Line large baking sheet with parchment paper. Heat 1 tablespoon butter in large skillet over high heat until foamy. Add plums; cook and stir about 3 minutes or until plums begin to break down. Stir in granulated sugar; cook 1 minute or until juices have thickened. Remove from heat; set aside.

2 Combine flour, oats, brown sugar, cinnamon and salt in medium bowl. Cut in remaining ¼ cup butter with pastry blender or 2 knives until mixture resembles coarse crumbs. Beat egg and water in small bowl.

3 Unroll pie crust on prepared baking sheet. Brush crust lightly with egg mixture. Sprinkle with ¼ cup oat mixture, leaving 2-inch border around edge of crust. Spoon plums over oat mixture, leaving juices in skillet. Sprinkle with crystallized ginger. Fold crust up around plums, overlapping as necessary. Sprinkle with remaining oat mixture. Brush edge of crust with egg mixture.

4 Bake 25 minutes or until golden brown. Cool slightly before serving.

# Perfect Pie Pastry

2¼ cups all-purpose flour

¾ teaspoon salt

½ cup shortening, well chilled

2 tablespoons butter, well chilled

5 to 6 tablespoons cold water

*Makes 8 servings (two 8- or 9-inch crusts)*

1 Place flour and salt in bowl of electric stand mixer. Turn to low and mix about 15 seconds. Cut shortening and butter into pieces and add to flour mixture. Continue mixing on low until shortening particles are size of small peas, 30 to 45 seconds.

2 Continuing on low, add water, 1 tablespoon at a time, mixing until ingredients are moistened and dough begins to hold together. Divide dough in half. Pat each half into a smooth ball and flatten slightly. Wrap in plastic wrap. Chill in refrigerator 15 minutes.

3 Roll one-half of dough to ⅛-inch thickness between sheets of waxed paper. Fold pastry into quarters. Ease into 8- or 9-inch pie plate and unfold, pressing firmly against bottom and sides.

For One-Crust Pie: Fold edge under. Crimp as desired. Add desired pie filling. Bake as directed.

For Two-Crust Pie: Trim pastry even with edge of pie plate. Using second half of dough, roll out another pastry crust. Add desired pie filling. Top with second pastry crust. Seal edge. Crimp as desired. Cut slits for steam to escape. Bake as directed.

For Baked Pastry Shell: Fold edge under. Crimp as desired. Prick sides and bottom with fork. Bake at 450°F for 8 to 10 minutes or until lightly browned. Cool completely on wire rack and fill.

Alternate Method for Baked Pastry Shell: Fold edge under. Crimp as desired. Line shell with foil. Fill with pie weights or dried beans. Bake at 450°F for 10 to 12 minutes or until edges are lightly browned. Remove pie weights and foil. Cool completely on wire rack and fill.

# Country Apple Tart

2½ pounds (about 6 large) tart green apples, peeled and thinly sliced

2 tablespoons lemon juice

¼ cup granulated sugar

⅓ cup packed light brown sugar

½ cup flour

½ teaspoon ground cinnamon

¼ cup butter, softened

1 (9-inch) Perfect Pie Pastry shell, unbaked (see recipe on page 200)

*Makes 8 servings*

1 Toss together apples, lemon juice and granulated sugar. Set aside. Place all remaining ingredients except Perfect Pie Pastry shell in bowl of electric stand mixer. Turn to low and mix until crumbly. Set aside.

2 Roll out pastry into 13-inch circle. Transfer to baking sheet (it's OK if pastry hangs over edge of baking sheet).

3 Gently mound apples in center of pastry, leaving 2-inch border of dough on all sides. Sprinkle apples with cinnamon sugar mixture. Fold pastry up over filling, pleating as necessary to fit snugly around apples. Gently press dough to filling, reinforcing shape.

4 Bake at 400°F until pastry is golden brown and apples are tender, about 30 minutes. Cool tart on baking sheet on wire rack 10 minutes; serve warm.

# Vanilla Cream Pie

1 cup sugar, divided

6 tablespoons all-purpose flour

$1/4$ teaspoon plus $1/8$ teaspoon salt, divided

$2^1/_2$ cups low-fat (1%) milk

3 eggs, separated

1 tablespoon butter

1 teaspoon vanilla

1 (9-inch) Perfect Pie Pastry shell, baked (see recipe on page 200)

$1/4$ teaspoon cream of tartar

*Makes 1 (9-inch) pie*

1 Combine $1/2$ cup sugar, flour and $1/4$ teaspoon salt in heavy saucepan. Add milk and cook over medium heat until thickened, stirring constantly. Reduce heat to low. Cook, covered, about 10 minutes longer, stirring occasionally. Set aside.

2 Place egg yolks in bowl of electric stand mixer. Turn to medium-high and whip about 1 minute. Slowly stir small amount of milk mixture into yolks. Add yolk mixture to saucepan. Cook over medium heat 3 to 4 minutes, stirring constantly. Remove from heat. Add butter and vanilla; cool. Pour into baked Pie Pastry shell.

3 Place cream of tartar, remaining salt and egg whites in mixer bowl. Gradually turn speed to medium-high and whip about 1 minute or until soft peaks form. Turn to medium-low. Gradually add remaining sugar and whip about 1 minute or until stiff peaks form.

4 Lightly pile egg white mixture on pie and spread to edge. Bake at 325°F for 15 minutes or until lightly browned.

Chocolate Cream Pie: Melt 2 squares (1 ounce each) unsweetened chocolate and add to filling along with butter and vanilla. Proceed as directed above.

Banana Cream Pie: Slice 2 or 3 bananas into baked Pie Pastry shell before adding filling. Proceed as directed above.

Coconut Cream Pie: Add $1/2$ cup flaked coconut to filling before pouring into baked Pie Pastry shell. Before baking, sprinkle $1/4$ cup flaked coconut on meringue. Proceed as directed above.

# Cherry Frangipane Tart

1 (9-inch) pie dough round

$^2/_3$ cup slivered almonds

$^1/_2$ cup all-purpose flour

$^1/_4$ cup powdered sugar

$^1/_2$ cup (1 stick) butter, softened

2 eggs

$1^3/_4$ cups whole frozen cherries, pitted*

*For best results, keep cherries frozen until ready to use.*

*Makes 6 to 8 servings*

1 Preheat oven to 450°F. Line tart pan with pie dough; cover with parchment paper. Fill paper-covered crust with weights (dried beans or other pie weights) and bake 10 minutes. Remove from oven. Carefully remove paper and weights. Reduce oven temperature to 350°F.

2 Combine almonds, flour and powdered sugar in bowl of food processor. Process until fine. Add butter; pulse to blend. Add eggs, 1 at a time, while processor is running.

3 Pour batter into baked crust; smooth top. Sprinkle with whole cherries. Bake about 35 minutes or until firm. Let cool at room temperature.

# Strawberry-Rhubarb Pie
## with Lattice Crust

2 cups (12 ounces) stemmed
and thickly sliced
strawberries

2 cups (8 ounces) diced
rhubarb

1 tablespoon orange juice

1¹/₂ cups sugar

3 tablespoons quick tapioca

¹/₈ teaspoon salt (optional)

1 recipe Pie Dough for a
2-Crust Pie (see recipe on
page 198)

1 tablespoon butter, cut into
small pieces

*Makes 1 pie*

1 Preheat oven to 375°F. Place strawberries and rhubarb together in medium bowl; sprinkle with orange juice. Stir sugar, tapioca and salt, if desired, together in small bowl. Stir sugar mixture into fruit until well combined; set aside.

2 Roll out one-half recipe of pie dough into 12-inch circle on lightly floured work surface. Fit into 9-inch pie pan. Trim all but ¹/₂ inch overhang and refrigerate dough-lined pan until needed.

3 Roll out second pastry disc into12-inch round. Cut round into 10 (³/₄-inch) strips.

4 Pour fruit mixture into chilled pie pan, dot top with butter pieces and lightly wet rim of pastry with wet pastry brush. Beginning with 2 longest pieces of dough, place 1 piece centered on pie and cross with second piece. Weave dough strips to form lattice crust working from pie's center. Trim edges of lattice top even with dough edge. Fold rim under and even with pan edge; gently press edges with tines of a fork to seal and create decorative edge.

5 Bake until crust is golden and fruit is bubbling, about 55 minutes. Transfer pie to wire rack; cool completely before serving.

# Chocolate **Pecan Pie**

4  eggs

1  cup sugar

1  cup dark corn syrup

3  squares (1 ounce each)
     unsweetened chocolate,
     melted

2  cups pecan halves

1  unbaked 10-inch pastry shell

*Makes 1 pie*

1 Place eggs, sugar and corn syrup in bowl of electric stand mixer.
Beat on medium-high 1 minute. Stop and scrape bowl.

2 Turn mixer to medium and gradually add chocolate; beat
1 minute or until well blended. Stir in pecans. Pour mixture into pastry
shell. Bake at 350°F for 35 to 45 minutes or until slightly soft in center.

# Orange Angel Pie

4 egg whites

1 1/2 teaspoons vanilla, divided

1 cup plus 2 teaspoons powdered sugar, divided

3/4 cup sugar

2 1/2 tablespoons cornstarch

1/8 teaspoon salt

3/4 cup orange juice

2 tablespoons grated fresh orange peel

2 tablespoons butter

1 cup heavy cream

*Makes 1 pie*

1 Place egg whites in bowl of electric stand mixer. Turn to medium-high and whip until foamy. Continuing on medium-high, add 1 teaspoon vanilla and gradually add 1 cup powdered sugar, beating until stiff but not dry. Spread mixture on bottom and sides of greased 9-inch glass pie plate. Bake at 225°F for 1 hour 15 minutes. Turn oven off and allow crust to cool with oven door ajar.

2 Combine sugar, cornstarch, salt and orange juice in small saucepan over medium heat. Cook and stir until well blended, then boil 1 minute. Remove mixture from heat and add orange peel and butter; blend well. Refrigerate mixture 15 minutes, and then pour into shell and refrigerate 1 to 2 hours.

3 Place remaining vanilla, remaining powdered sugar and cream in mixer bowl. Turn mixer to medium-high and whip until stiff. Spread whipped cream on pie and serve immediately.

# Bourbon-Laced Sweet Potato Pie

1 pound (2 medium) sweet
   potatoes, peeled and cut
   into 1-inch chunks

2 tablespoons butter

³/₄ cup packed brown sugar

1 teaspoon ground cinnamon

¹/₄ teaspoon salt

2 eggs

³/₄ cup whipping cream

¹/₄ cup bourbon or whiskey

1 (9-inch) Perfect Pie Pastry
   shell, unbaked (see recipe
   on page 200)

   Sweetened whipped cream

**TIP**

*Pie can be cooled completely,
covered and chilled up to 24 hours
before serving. Let stand at room
temperature at least 30 minutes
before serving.*

*Makes 1 pie*

1 Preheat oven to 350°F. Place sweet potatoes in saucepan; cover with
water. Simmer until very tender, about 20 minutes. Drain well in
colander; transfer to large bowl of electric stand mixer. Add butter; beat
at medium until smooth. Add brown sugar, cinnamon and salt; beat until
smooth. Beat in eggs 1 at a time. Beat in cream and bourbon.

2 Line 9-inch pie plate (not deep-dish) with pastry; flute edges. Pour
sweet potato mixture into crust. Bake 50 minutes or until knife
inserted near center comes out clean. Transfer to wire rack; cool at least
1 hour before serving. Serve warm or at room temperature topped with
whipped cream.

# Key Lime Pie

2 cups sugar, divided

$\frac{1}{4}$ cup plus 2 tablespoons cornstarch

$\frac{1}{4}$ teaspoon salt

$\frac{1}{2}$ cup fresh key lime juice*

$\frac{1}{2}$ cup cold water

3 eggs, separated

2 tablespoons butter

$1\frac{1}{2}$ cups boiling water

1 teaspoon grated fresh lime peel

Green food coloring (optional)

$\frac{1}{4}$ teaspoon cream of tartar

1 (9-inch) Perfect Pie Pastry shell, baked (see recipe on page 200)

*Bottled key lime juice may be substituted for fresh key lime juice.*

*Makes 1 pie*

1 Combine $1\frac{1}{2}$ cups sugar, cornstarch and salt in 2-quart saucepan. Add lime juice, water and egg yolks; blend well. Add butter, and gradually add boiling water. Bring mixture to a boil over medium heat and cook 3 minutes, stirring constantly. Stir in lime peel and green food coloring, if desired. Remove from heat and cool 20 minutes.

2 Beat egg whites in bowl of electric stand mixer on high until frothy. Add cream of tartar and whip until soft peaks form. Continuing on high, gradually add remaining sugar, beating until stiff peaks form.

3 Pour cooled filling into pie shell. Lightly pile meringue on filling and spread to edges. Bake at 350°F for 15 minutes or until lightly browned. Cool completely before serving.

# Raspberry Cream Pie

## Crust

1⅓ cups ground pecans

2 tablespoons melted butter

1 tablespoon sucralose-based sugar substitute

¼ teaspoon ground cinnamon

## Filling

½ cup water

1 envelope unflavored gelatin

6 tablespoons powdered sugar

¼ cup sucralose-based sugar substitute

1 tablespoon fresh lemon juice

⅛ teaspoon salt

2 cups fresh raspberries or 1 bag (12 ounces) frozen unsweetened raspberries, thawed

1 cup heavy cream

*Makes 1 pie*

1 Preheat oven to 350°F. Combine ground pecans, melted butter, sugar substitute and cinnamon in medium bowl. Press into bottom and up sides of 9-inch pie plate. Bake 5 to 7 minutes or until set and lightly browned. Cool completely.

2 Pour ½ cup water into medium saucepan; sprinkle with gelatin. Let stand about 5 minutes or until gelatin is softened. Add powdered sugar, sugar substitute, lemon juice and salt to gelatin mixture. Cook and stir over medium-low heat until sugar and gelatin are completely dissolved. Stir in raspberries. Let stand about 30 minutes or until thickened.

3 Beat cream in large bowl of electric stand mixer at high until stiff peaks form. Fold in raspberry mixture. Gently spoon into prepared crust. Refrigerate 2 to 3 hours before serving.

# Quick and Creamy
# Strawberry-Banana Tart

1 package (16 ounces) frozen unsweetened whole strawberries, thawed

2 tablespoons plus 1 1/2 teaspoons frozen orange juice concentrate, thawed and divided

1/4 cup sugar

1 envelope unflavored gelatin

3 egg whites, beaten

1 package (3 ounces) soft ladyfingers, split

4 teaspoons water

1/2 container (8 ounces) reduced-fat, nondairy frozen whipped topping, thawed

1 medium banana, quartered lengthwise and sliced

1 teaspoon multicolored decorator sprinkles (optional)

*Makes 1 tart*

1 Place thawed strawberries and 2 tablespoons orange juice concentrate in blender container or food processor bowl. Blend or process until smooth.

2 Stir together sugar and gelatin in medium saucepan. Stir in strawberry mixture. Cook, stirring frequently, until boiling.

3 Stir about half of mixture into beaten egg whites. Return mixture to saucepan. Cook, stirring constantly, over medium heat about 2 minutes or until slightly thickened. (Do not boil.)

4 Pour into bowl. Refrigerate 2 to 2 1/2 hours or until mixture mounds when spooned, stirring occasionally.

5 Cut half of ladyfingers in half horizontally. Place around edge of 9-inch tart pan with removable bottom. Place remaining ladyfingers into bottom of pan, cutting to fit.

6 Stir together remaining 1 1/2 teaspoons orange juice concentrate and water. Drizzle over ladyfingers.

7 Fold thawed whipped topping and banana into strawberry mixture. Spoon into ladyfinger crust. Refrigerate at least 2 hours. Sprinkle with multicolored sprinkles, if desired. Cut into 10 wedges to serve.

# Country Pear Pie

3/4 cup brown sugar

3 tablespoons all-purpose
   flour

1/8 teaspoon salt

   Dash ground cloves

   Dash ground nutmeg

1/3 cup heavy cream

2 tablespoons lemon juice

8 to 10 medium pears (about
   2 1/2 pounds) pared, cored
   and thinly sliced

2 tablespoons butter

   Two-Crust Perfect Pie Pastry
   shell, unbaked (see recipe
   on page 200)

*Makes 1 pie*

1 Combine brown sugar, flour, salt, cloves and nutmeg in small bowl. Stir in cream. In another bowl, sprinkle lemon juice over pears. Add brown sugar and cream mixture and mix well. Set aside.

2 Divide pastry in half. Roll to 1/8-inch thickness and line 9-inch pie plate. Fill with pear mixture and dot with butter. Roll out remaining pastry and cut into 1/2-inch strips. Weave strips into lattice on top of pears. Seal and crimp edges. Bake at 400°F for 35 to 40 minutes.

# Plum-Topped Custard Tartlets

1 cup half-and-half

2 eggs

1 tablespoon all-purpose flour

$^1/_2$ cup plus 1 tablespoon
   granulated sugar, divided

$^1/_2$ teaspoon vanilla

$^1/_2$ cup whipping cream

1 package (10 ounces) frozen
   puff pastry shells (6 shells),
   baked according to package
   directions

1 tablespoon butter

2 large firm red plums,
   unpeeled, halved, pitted
   and sliced into thin wedges

1 tablespoon packed brown
   sugar

*Makes 6 servings*

1 Heat half-and-half to a simmer in saucepan over medium heat. Beat eggs, flour and $^1/_2$ cup sugar in heatproof bowl. Gradually pour $^1/_2$ cup half-and-half into egg mixture, beating constantly. Pour egg mixture back into saucepan with remaining half-and-half. Cook 7 to 8 minutes, stirring constantly until mixture is consistency of pudding. Remove from heat and stir in vanilla. Pour through strainer into bowl. Chill custard until thick.

2 Beat whipping cream in bowl of electric stand mixer at medium-high until soft peaks form. Add remaining 1 tablespoon sugar and beat until stiff. Fold chilled custard into cream. Spoon custard mixture into pastry shells. Refrigerate remaining custard.

3 Melt butter in medium skillet, and then add plum wedges. Cook 2 minutes or until plums become slightly pulpy. Stir in brown sugar and cook 1 minute longer. Arrange a few plum slices over each tartlet.

**Spinach Salad with Goat Cheese Stuffed Mushrooms** *(recipe on page 220)*

# salads and. dressings

Healthy, fresh, and fast, salads have emerged as dishes worthy of main-course status. A bowl of leafy greens topped with fresh vegetables and a simple dressing is the perfect solution for the health-conscious, time-constrained cook.

These salads spotlight the possibilities of fresh produce and show how even "health food" can be adventurous, flavorful, and completely satisfying.

# Spinach Salad with Goat Cheese Stuffed Mushrooms

*(photo on page 218)*

5 ounces baby spinach
   or 1 bunch spinach, washed
   and dried

4 tablespoons olive oil

3 tablespoons balsamic vinegar

2 teaspoons chopped shallots

1/4 teaspoon salt

8 baby portobello or large
   cremini mushrooms

2 teaspoons honey

4 ounces herbed goat cheese

2 tablespoons cream cheese

4 tablespoons sliced or slivered
   toasted almonds

*Makes 4 servings*

1 Arrange spinach on large platter or individual serving plates. Combine olive oil, vinegar, shallots and salt in small bowl or covered jar; mix well. Remove stems from mushrooms. Drizzle 2 tablespoons oil mixture over mushroom caps, gill-side up, and let marinate 15 to 30 minutes. Add honey to remaining oil mixture; set aside.

2 Combine goat cheese and cream cheese in small bowl and set aside to soften.

3 Preheat oven to 400°F. Put mushrooms in baking dish gill-side down and bake 10 minutes. Turn mushrooms over; stuff each with about 1 tablespoon goat cheese mixture. Bake 5 to 10 minutes more until cheese is warm and soft.

4 Remove cooked mushrooms from pan. Pour cooking liquid into dressing. Pour half of dressing over spinach and toss. Arrange cooked mushrooms on salad. Drizzle remaining dressing over mushrooms. Sprinkle with almonds.

# Rustic Dried Cherry Salad

3 cups French bread, diced
(see recipe on page 57)

¹/₄ cup pecans, chopped

¹/₂ cup dried sweetened
cherries, chopped

1 celery stalk, trimmed and
diced

3 tablespoons canola oil or
1¹/₂ tablespoons canola oil
and 1¹/₂ tablespoons olive
oil

3 tablespoons raspberry
vinegar

1 tablespoon honey

2 tablespoons water

¹/₄ teaspoon curry powder

*Makes 4 servings*

1 Toast bread in 350°F oven 15 minutes. Cool completely.
Set aside.

2 Toast pecans in preheated skillet over medium heat 3 minutes,
stirring frequently.

3 Combine pecans, cherries, celery and bread in large salad bowl.
Combine oil, vinegar, honey, water and curry powder in cup.
Stir well. Pour over salad and toss. Serve immediately.

# French Lentil **Salad**

2 quarts water

1¹/₂ cups dried lentils, sorted, rinsed and drained*

¹/₄ cup chopped walnuts

4 green onions, finely chopped

3 tablespoons balsamic vinegar

2 tablespoons chopped fresh parsley

1 tablespoon olive oil

³/₄ teaspoon salt

¹/₂ teaspoon dried thyme

¹/₄ teaspoon black pepper

Lettuce leaves (optional)

*Packages of dried lentils may contain dirt and tiny stones. So thoroughly rinse lentils, and then sort through them and discard any unusual-looking pieces.*

*Makes 4 servings*

1 Combine water and lentils in large saucepan; bring to a boil over high heat. Cover; reduce heat and simmer 30 minutes or until lentils are tender, stirring occasionally. Drain lentils; discard liquid.

2 Meanwhile, preheat oven to 375°F. Spread walnuts in even layer on baking sheet. Bake 5 minutes or until lightly browned. Cool completely on baking sheet.

3 Combine lentils, onions, vinegar, parsley, oil, salt, thyme and pepper in large bowl. Cover; refrigerate 1 hour or until cool.

4 Serve on lettuce leaves, if desired. Top with toasted walnuts before serving.

# Grilled Chicken **Caesar Salad**

1 pound boneless, skinless chicken breast halves

1/2 cup extra-virgin olive oil

3 tablespoons fresh lemon juice

2 teaspoons anchovy paste

2 cloves garlic, minced

1/2 teaspoon salt

1/2 teaspoon black pepper

6 cups torn romaine lettuce leaves

4 plum tomatoes, quartered

1/4 cup grated Parmesan cheese

1 cup garlic croutons

*Makes 4 servings*

1 Place chicken in large resealable food storage bag. Combine oil, lemon juice, anchovy paste, garlic, salt and pepper in small bowl. Reserve 1/3 cup marinade; cover and refrigerate until serving. Pour remaining marinade over chicken in bag. Seal bag tightly, turning to coat. Marinate in refrigerator at least 1 hour or up to 4 hours, turning occasionally.

2 Combine lettuce, tomatoes and cheese in large bowl. Cover; refrigerate until serving.

3 Prepare grill for direct cooking. Drain chicken, pouring marinade into small saucepan. Bring marinade to a boil; boil 1 minute.

4 Place chicken on grid. Grill chicken, on covered grill, over medium coals 10 to 12 minutes or until chicken is no longer pink in center, brushing with marinade after 5 minutes and turning halfway through grilling time. Discard remaining marinade. Cool chicken slightly.

5 Slice warm chicken crosswise into 1/2-inch-wide strips; add chicken and croutons to lettuce mixture in bowl. Drizzle with 1/3 cup reserved marinade; toss to coat well.

# Marinated Tomato Salad

1½ cups tarragon vinegar or
    white wine vinegar

½ teaspoon salt

¼ cup finely chopped shallots

2 tablespoons finely chopped
    chives

2 tablespoons fresh lemon
    juice

¼ teaspoon white pepper

2 tablespoons extra-virgin
    olive oil

6 plum tomatoes, quartered

2 large yellow tomatoes,*
    sliced into ½-inch-thick
    slices

16 red cherry tomatoes, halved

16 small yellow pear tomatoes,*
    halved (optional)

Sunflower sprouts (optional)

*Substitute 10 plum tomatoes, quartered
vertically, for yellow tomatoes and yellow
pear tomatoes, if desired.

*Makes 8 servings*

1 Combine vinegar and salt in large bowl; stir until salt is completely
dissolved. Add shallots, chives, lemon juice and pepper; mix well.
Slowly whisk in oil until well blended.

2 Add tomatoes to marinade; toss well. Cover; let stand at room
temperature 30 minutes.

3 To serve, place 3 plum tomato quarters on each of 8 salad plates.
Add 2 slices yellow tomato, 4 cherry tomato halves and 4 pear tomato
halves, if desired. Garnish with sunflower sprouts.

# Blue Cheese Dressing

1 cup mayonnaise
2/3 cup crumbled blue cheese
2 tablespoons lemon juice
1/4 teaspoon black pepper

*Makes 2 cups*

Place all ingredients in bowl of electric stand mixer. Turn mixer to low and mix 1 minute. Chill thoroughly before serving.

# Russian Dressing

1 cup mayonnaise
1/2 cup ketchup
2 drops hot pepper sauce
1/4 cup chopped fresh parsley
Salt and black pepper

*Makes 1 1/2 cups*

Place all ingredients in bowl of electric stand mixer. Turn to low and mix 1 minute. Chill thoroughly before serving.

# Poppy Seed Dressing

1/4 cup sugar
1/3 cup cider vinegar
1 teaspoon dry mustard
1 teaspoon minced onion
1 teaspoon salt
1 cup vegetable oil
1 1/2 teaspoons poppy seeds

*Makes 1 1/2 cups*

1 Place sugar, vinegar, dry mustard, onion and salt in bowl of electric stand mixer. Turn to medium-low and whip 2 minutes.

2 Increase speed to medium-high and slowly add oil in thin, steady stream until completely absorbed. Reduce to low; add poppy seeds, mixing just until combined. Chill thoroughly before serving.

# Market Salad

3 eggs

4 cups washed mixed baby
   salad greens

2 cups green beans, cut into
   1¹/₂-inch pieces, cooked
   and drained

4 thick slices bacon, crisp-
   cooked and crumbled

1 tablespoon minced fresh
   basil, chives or Italian
   parsley

3 tablespoons olive oil

1 tablespoon red wine vinegar

1 teaspoon Dijon mustard

¹/₄ teaspoon salt

¹/₄ teaspoon black pepper

*Makes 4 servings*

1 Place eggs in small saucepan with water to cover; bring to a boil over medium-high heat. Immediately remove from heat. Cover; let stand 10 minutes. Drain; cool eggs to room temperature.

2 Combine salad greens, green beans, bacon and basil in large serving bowl. Peel and coarsely chop eggs; add to serving bowl. Combine oil, vinegar, mustard, salt and pepper in small bowl; drizzle over salad. Toss gently to coat.

**salads and dressings** |

Kansas City Barbecue Sauce *(recipe on page 231)*

# sides
## and
# sauces

Sweet and tangy barbecue sauce
is the crowning glory for a slab of ribs, and a pot
roast isn't complete without a buttery mound
of mashed potatoes.

Sides and sauces are often the key to delicious
dining. Complement the flavors and textures of your
entrées with these perfect counterparts to create
an exquisite menu for any occasion.

# Stuffed Eggplant

3 medium eggplants, trimmed

2 small onions, quartered

2 cloves garlic

$^1/_4$ cup olive oil

$^3/_4$ cup long-grain rice

1 can (10$^3/_4$ ounces) chicken broth or fat-free reduced-sodium chicken broth

1 teaspoon sugar

$^1/_2$ teaspoon dried basil

$^1/_2$ teaspoon salt

$^1/_2$ teaspoon black pepper

Dash ground cinnamon

2 tomatoes, diced

$^1/_2$ cup grated Parmesan cheese

2 tablespoons butter, melted

## TIP

*When selecting eggplants, they should be firm with a shiny, smooth purple skin.*

*Makes 6 servings*

1 Cut eggplants in half lengthwise. Scoop out pulp, leaving $^3/_8$-inch shell; set aside.

2 Place eggplant pulp, onions and garlic in food processor and pulse until coarsely ground.

3 Heat oil in 12-inch skillet over medium heat. Add ground vegetables; cook and stir 4 minutes. Add rice, chicken broth, sugar, basil, salt, pepper and cinnamon; mix well. Cover and simmer over low heat 15 minutes. Add tomatoes and simmer 10 minutes more.

4 Remove mixture from heat and stir in Parmesan cheese. Loosely stuff each eggplant shell. Place shells in greased 13×9×2-inch pan.

5 Brush eggplants with butter. Cover and bake at 325°F for 20 minutes. Remove cover and bake 30 minutes more or until tops are crusty. Serve immediately.

**sides and sauces**

# Herbed Whipped Squash

1 large butternut squash, baked (about 3 cups cooked)
1/4 cup butter, melted
1/2 teaspoon dried tarragon
1/8 teaspoon salt
1/8 teaspoon black pepper

*Makes 6 servings*

Scoop cooked squash out of shell and place in bowl of electric stand mixer. Turn mixer to medium-low and beat about 30 seconds. Add all remaining ingredients. Turn to low and mix about 30 seconds. Turn to medium-low and beat 2 minutes more.

# Kansas City Barbecue Sauce

*(photo on page 228)*

1 1/2 cups ketchup
1/3 cup packed light brown sugar
1/4 cup molasses
1/4 cup cider vinegar
1 tablespoon dry mustard
2 teaspoons onion powder
2 teaspoons chili powder
1 teaspoon paprika
1 teaspoon garlic powder
1 teaspoon ground cumin
1/4 teaspoon ground allspice
1/8 teaspoon ground red pepper

*Makes 2 cups*

Combine all ingredients in medium saucepan over medium-high heat. Bring to a boil, stirring to dissolve sugar; cover and reduce heat to medium-low. Simmer, stirring occasionally, 20 minutes or until slightly thickened.

# Orange and Maple Glazed Roasted Beets

4   medium beets, scrubbed
2   teaspoons olive oil
1/4 cup freshly squeezed orange
    juice
2   teaspoons grated orange
    peel
3   tablespoons balsamic or
    cider vinegar
1   teaspoon Dijon mustard
2   tablespoons maple syrup
    Salt and black pepper
1   to 2 tablespoons chopped
    fresh mint (optional)

*Makes 4 servings*

1 Preheat oven to 425°F. Rub beets with olive oil and place in glass baking dish. Cover and bake 45 minutes to 1 hour or until a knife inserted into the largest beet goes in easily. Remove beets from oven and let cool. When cooled, peel and cut in half lengthwise. Lay flat side down and cut beets into slices.

2 Place sliced beets in glass baking dish. Combine orange juice and half the zest, vinegar, mustard and maple syrup in small bowl. Mix to combine and pour over beets. Return beets to oven until they are hot and have absorbed marinade, about 10 to 15 minutes. Remove from oven and place on serving platter. Sprinkle with remaining peel, salt, pepper and mint.

# Green Beans and Shiitake Mushrooms

10 to 12 dried shiitake
    mushrooms (about
    1 ounce)

$3/4$ cup water, divided

3 tablespoons oyster sauce

1 tablespoon cornstarch

4 cloves garlic, minced

$1/8$ teaspoon red pepper flakes

1 tablespoon vegetable oil

$3/4$ to 1 pound fresh green
    beans, ends trimmed

$1/3$ cup slivered fresh basil or
    chopped fresh cilantro

2 green onions, sliced
    diagonally

$1/3$ cup roasted peanuts
    (optional)

*Makes 4 to 6 servings*

1 Place mushrooms in bowl; cover with hot water. Let stand 30 minutes or until caps are soft. Drain mushrooms; squeeze out excess water. Remove and discard stems. Slice caps into thin strips.

2 Combine $1/4$ cup water, oyster sauce, cornstarch, garlic and red pepper in small bowl; mix well. Set aside.

3 Heat wok or medium skillet over medium-high heat. Add oil and swirl to coat surface. Add mushrooms, beans and remaining $1/2$ cup water; cook and stir until water boils. Reduce heat to medium-low; cover and cook 8 to 10 minutes or until beans are crisp-tender, stirring occasionally.

4 Stir cornstarch mixture; add to wok. Cook and stir until sauce thickens and coats beans. (If cooking water has evaporated, add enough water to form thick sauce.) Stir in basil, green onions and peanuts, if desired; mix well. Transfer to serving platter.

# Sweet Potato Puff

2 medium sweet potatoes,
cooked and peeled

$1/2$ cup low-fat (1%) milk

$1/3$ cup sugar

2 eggs

2 tablespoons butter

$1/2$ teaspoon ground nutmeg

$1/2$ teaspoon ground cinnamon

Crunchy Praline Topping
(recipe follows)

*Makes 6 servings ($1/2$ cup per serving)*

1 Place potatoes in bowl of electric stand mixer. Turn to low and mix about 30 seconds. Add milk, sugar, eggs, butter, nutmeg and cinnamon. Turn to medium-low and beat 1 minute.

2 Spread mixture in greased 9-inch pie plate. Bake at 400°F for 20 minutes or until set. Prepare Crunchy Praline Topping while puff bakes. Spread Crunchy Praline Topping on hot puff. Bake 10 minutes longer.

## Crunchy Praline Topping

2 tablespoons butter, melted

$3/4$ cup cornflake cereal

$1/2$ cup chopped walnuts or pecans

$1/4$ cup firmly packed brown sugar

Place all ingredients in bowl of electric stand mixer. Turn mixer to low and mix about 15 seconds.

# Stuffed New Potatoes

8 small new red potatoes,
boiled in their skins

1/4 cup reduced-fat sour cream

1 tablespoon butter, melted

1/4 teaspoon garlic salt

1/4 teaspoon dried thyme

1/4 cup finely chopped green
onions

1/4 cup finely shredded Cheddar
cheese

Paprika (optional)

*Makes 8 servings (2 potato halves per serving)*

1 Cut potatoes in half. Scoop out insides of potatoes, leaving 1/8-inch shells. Place insides of potatoes in bowl of electric stand mixer. Turn mixer to low and mix about 1 minute. Add sour cream, butter, garlic salt and thyme. Turn to medium-low and mix about 30 seconds. Turn to low and add onions, mixing just until blended.

2 Spoon or pipe potato mixture into potato shells. Place filled shells in shallow baking dish. Bake at 375°F for 20 to 25 minutes or until thoroughly heated. Sprinkle with cheese and paprika, if desired. Bake 5 minutes longer or until cheese is melted. Serve warm.

# Bacon Swiss Potatoes

6 slices bacon

1 medium onion, peeled and chopped

8 ounces finely shredded Swiss cheese, divided

4 eggs, beaten

³/₄ cup heavy cream

¹/₄ teaspoon ground nutmeg

¹/₂ teaspoon salt

¹/₄ teaspoon black pepper

1 clove garlic, minced

3 to 4 potatoes, peeled and coarsely shredded

*Makes 6 to 8 servings*

1 Fry bacon in 12-inch skillet over medium-high heat until very crisp. Remove from pan and crumble. Drain all but ¹/₄ cup bacon fat. Add onion and cook and stir 3 minutes; remove from heat and set aside.

2 Combine 2 cups shredded cheese, eggs, heavy cream, nutmeg, salt, pepper and garlic in medium saucepan. Cook over low heat, stirring occasionally, until cheese melts. Do not boil. Stir in potatoes and onion; mix well.

3 Pour half of cheese/potato mixture into greased 9×9×1¹/₂-inch pan. Sprinkle half of bacon over mixture. Repeat with remaining cheese/potato mixture and bacon. Top with remaining cheese. Bake at 400°F for 45 to 50 minutes or until bubbly and golden brown. Serve immediately.

# Braised Red Cabbage

1 small head red cabbage, cored and thinly sliced

1/4 cup sugar

1 tablespoon salt

1 cup red wine vinegar

1/4 cup (1/2 stick) butter

1 onion, peeled and thinly sliced

1 apple, peeled, cored and diced

1/2 cup red currant jelly

1/4 cup hot water

1/8 teaspoon ground cloves

1/4 teaspoon ground cinnamon

*Makes 6 to 8 servings*

1 Combine cabbage, sugar, salt and vinegar in large bowl; marinate 15 minutes.

2 Melt butter in 5-quart pot over medium heat. Add onion and cook and stir 5 minutes or until transparent. Add apple and cook and stir 5 minutes more. Add cabbage mixture to pot and bring to a boil; reduce heat.

3 Combine jelly, hot water, cloves and cinnamon. Add to cabbage mixture. Cover and simmer 1 hour or until tender. Serve immediately.

# Spinach Soufflé

2 packages (10 ounces each) frozen chopped spinach, cooked

¼ cup butter

1 tablespoon minced onion

5 tablespoons flour

1 cup milk

¼ pound Cheddar cheese, shredded

1 teaspoon salt

¼ teaspoon black pepper

⅛ teaspoon ground nutmeg

3 eggs, separated

*Makes 4 to 6 servings*

1 Wring spinach in towel until very dry. Place spinach in food processor and pulse until coarsely chopped; set aside.

2 Melt butter in saucepan over medium heat. Add onion and cook and stir 5 minutes. Blend in flour, and then gradually add milk, stirring until smooth. Continue cooking until thickened, about 5 minutes. Remove mixture from heat and stir in spinach, cheese, salt, pepper and nutmeg; set aside.

3 Place egg whites in bowl of electric stand mixer. Turn to medium-high and whip until stiff but not dry. Remove egg whites from bowl. Clean mixer bowl.

4 Place egg yolks in mixer bowl. Turn speed to medium-low and whip egg yolks until thick, about 1 minute.

5 Fold spinach and cheese mixture into beaten egg whites, and then fold in beaten egg yolks. Pour in greased 1½-quart souffle dish and bake at 350°F for 45 to 50 minutes. Serve immediately.

# Mediterranean Potato Casserole

3 tablespoons olive oil, divided

3 medium Yukon Gold or Yellow Finn potatoes, peeled

1 medium sweet potato, peeled

2 to 3 teaspoons herbes de Provence

1 teaspoon coarse or Kosher salt

$1/2$ cup vegetable or chicken broth

3 tablespoons shredded Asiago or Parmesan cheese

*Makes 4 servings*

1 Preheat oven to 425°F. Pour 1 tablespoon olive oil in bottom of 8-inch square glass baking pan or ceramic dish to cover bottom of pan.

2 Slice yellow potatoes in food processor with 3-millimeter slicing blade. Remove and set aside. Slice sweet potatoes and set aside.

3 Make 1 layer of yellow potatoes in bottom of dish. Lightly drizzle with olive oil; sprinkle with about 1 teaspoon herbs and salt. Repeat, alternating layers of sweet potatoes and yellow potatoes. Pour broth over top layer; sprinkle with herbs and cover pan.

4 Bake 30 minutes. Remove cover. Drizzle top with about 1 teaspoon olive oil and sprinkle cheese on top.

5 Broil 3 minutes until cheese sizzles. Remove from oven and let sit 5 minutes before serving.

# Red Pepper Relish

2 large tomatoes, cut into eighths

2 stalks celery, cut into 1-inch pieces

3 red peppers, seeded and cut into eighths

1 onion, quartered

1 tablespoon salt

2 tablespoons sugar

$\frac{1}{8}$ teaspoon ground allspice

$\frac{1}{8}$ teaspoon ground cinnamon

$\frac{1}{8}$ teaspoon ground cloves

$\frac{1}{4}$ cup red wine vinegar

*Makes 4 cups*

1 Run tomatoes through food mill into large glass bowl; set aside.

2 Place celery, peppers and onion in food processor; pulse until coarsely ground. Pour pepper mixture into bowl with tomato mixture. Add salt, sugar, allspice, cinnamon, cloves and vinegar; mix well.

3 Cover and refrigerate, stirring occasionally, at least 8 hours before serving.

**To sterilize jars:** Wash jars in hot, sudsy water and rinse well. Put jars in a large kettle and cover with hot water. Bring to a boil and boil for 15 minutes. Turn off heat and let jars stand in hot water until ready to fill. Sterilize lids for 5 minutes or according to manufacturer's directions.

# Cheese Sauce

2 tablespoons butter

2 tablespoons all-purpose flour

$1\frac{1}{2}$ cups milk, divided

$\frac{1}{8}$ teaspoon ground nutmeg

$\frac{1}{4}$ teaspoon black pepper

$\frac{1}{4}$ teaspoon salt

$\frac{1}{4}$ teaspoon dry mustard

8 ounces shredded Cheddar cheese

2 teaspoons dry sherry

*Makes 2 cups*

1 Melt butter in large saucepan over medium heat. Blend in flour and stir 2 minutes. Gradually add 1 cup milk, stirring until smooth.

2 Add nutmeg, pepper, salt and dry mustard and stir another minute. Add shredded cheese to mixture, stirring until melted. Add remaining milk and sherry and cook 2 minutes. Serve immediately.

# Horseradish **Sauce**

1 cup heavy cream

3 tablespoons horseradish

$^1/_4$ teaspoon salt

$^1/_4$ cup chopped fresh parsley

*Makes 2 cups*

Place cream in bowl of electric stand mixer. Turn mixer to medium-high and whip until stiff peaks form. Reduce to low; add horseradish, salt and parsley, mixing just until combined. Serve immediately.

# Tangy Tailgate **Cole Slaw**

1 small head cabbage (1$^1/_2$ to 2 pounds)

$^1/_2$ cup shredded carrots

$^1/_2$ cup mayonnaise

$^1/_2$ cup sour cream

$^1/_4$ to $^1/_3$ cup creamy horseradish sauce

2 to 3 tablespoons granulated sugar

$^3/_4$ teaspoon salt

$^1/_2$ teaspoon celery salt

$^1/_4$ teaspoon dry mustard

*Makes 8 servings*

1 Core cabbage; cut into large chunks. Process in batches in food processor until cabbage is finely chopped. Transfer to a large transportable bowl with cover. (Do not wash food processor.) Stir carrots into cabbage.

2 Add remaining ingredients to food processor; process until well combined. Adjust horseradish and sugar to taste. Pour mixture over cabbage; toss well. Cover; chill at least 8 hours or up to 24 hours.

# Southern-Style Collard Greens

8 slices hickory smoked bacon

1 large onion, chopped

1 teaspoon sugar

3 cloves garlic, minced

$1/8$ teaspoon red pepper flakes

2 tablespoons cider vinegar

3 pounds fresh collard greens, washed and chopped, thick stems removed

1 ($14^{1}/_2$-ounce) can fat-free reduced-sodium chicken broth

$1/2$ teaspoon salt

$1/4$ teaspoon black pepper

*Makes 4 servings*

1 Cook bacon in large Dutch oven over medium heat until crisp, 8 to 9 minutes. Transfer to plate covered with paper towels and drain well. Crumble bacon; set aside.

2 Pour off all but 3 tablespoons bacon fat and return Dutch oven to stove. Add onion and sugar; cook 5 to 6 minutes until onions begin to lightly brown, stirring occasionally. Add garlic and red pepper flakes and cook 1 minute more. Add vinegar and cook 45 seconds. Stir in collard greens and cook, stirring, until wilted, about 3 minutes. Add 6 slices of crumbled bacon, broth, salt and pepper.

3 Bring to a boil. Cover and reduce heat to medium-low. Simmer until greens are very tender, about 45 minutes. Divide among 4 plates and top each with reserved crumbled bacon.

# Spicy Creole Sauce

2 tablespoons olive oil

1 large onion, diced

1 large green pepper, seeded and diced

3 celery stalks, diced

3/4 cup tomato purée*

1 cup sliced mushrooms

2 large tomatoes, seeded and diced

1 bay leaf

3 drops hot pepper sauce

*Or substitute 3 large tomatoes cut into sixths and run through a food mill.

*Makes 2½ cups*

1 Heat oil in 12-inch skillet over medium-high heat. Add onion, green pepper and celery. Cook and stir about 5 minutes or until transparent.

2 Add tomato purée, mushrooms, diced tomatoes, bay leaf and hot pepper sauce. Reduce heat; cover and simmer 20 minutes. Remove bay leaf before serving. Use sauce as topping for baked fish or poultry or as an omelet filling.

# Rémoulade Sauce

1 cup mayonnaise

3 tablespoons chopped capers

1 tablespoon chopped dill pickle

1/2 teaspoon dried tarragon

1/2 teaspoon dried chervil

1/4 teaspoon salt

1/4 teaspoon black pepper

2 teaspoons Dijon–style mustard

*Makes 1 cup*

Place all ingredients in bowl of electric stand mixer. Turn to medium-low and whip 1 minute. Chill thoroughly before serving.

# Index

## Cookies, Bars and Candies

## Desserts

## Fish and Seafood

## Salads and Dressings

## Sides and Sauces

## Vegetarian

# METRIC CONVERSION CHART

## VOLUME MEASUREMENTS (dry)

$\frac{1}{8}$ teaspoon = 0.5 mL
$\frac{1}{4}$ teaspoon = 1 mL
$\frac{1}{2}$ teaspoon = 2 mL
$\frac{3}{4}$ teaspoon = 4 mL
1 teaspoon = 5 mL
1 tablespoon = 15 mL
2 tablespoons = 30 mL
$\frac{1}{4}$ cup = 60 mL
$\frac{1}{3}$ cup = 75 mL
$\frac{1}{2}$ cup = 125 mL
$\frac{2}{3}$ cup = 150 mL
$\frac{3}{4}$ cup = 175 mL
1 cup = 250 mL
2 cups = 1 pint = 500 mL
3 cups = 750 mL
4 cups = 1 quart = 1 L

## VOLUME MEASUREMENTS (fluid)

1 fluid ounce (2 tablespoons) = 30 mL
4 fluid ounces ($\frac{1}{2}$ cup) = 125 mL
8 fluid ounces (1 cup) = 250 mL
12 fluid ounces (1$\frac{1}{2}$ cups) = 375 mL
16 fluid ounces (2 cups) = 500 mL

## WEIGHTS (mass)

$\frac{1}{2}$ ounce = 15 g
1 ounce = 30 g
3 ounces = 90 g
4 ounces = 120 g
8 ounces = 225 g
10 ounces = 285 g
12 ounces = 360 g
16 ounces = 1 pound = 450 g

## DIMENSIONS

$\frac{1}{16}$ inch = 2 mm
$\frac{1}{8}$ inch = 3 mm
$\frac{1}{4}$ inch = 6 mm
$\frac{1}{2}$ inch = 1.5 cm
$\frac{3}{4}$ inch = 2 cm
1 inch = 2.5 cm

## OVEN TEMPERATURES

250°F = 120°C
275°F = 140°C
300°F = 150°C
325°F = 160°C
350°F = 180°C
375°F = 190°C
400°F = 200°C
425°F = 220°C
450°F = 230°C

## BAKING PAN SIZES

| Utensil | Size in Inches/Quarts | Metric Volume | Size in Centimeters |
|---|---|---|---|
| Baking or Cake Pan (square or rectangular) | 8×8×2 | 2 L | 20×20×5 |
| | 9×9×2 | 2.5 L | 23×23×5 |
| | 12×8×2 | 3 L | 30×20×5 |
| | 13×9×2 | 3.5 L | 33×23×5 |
| Loaf Pan | 8×4×3 | 1.5 L | 20×10×7 |
| | 9×5×3 | 2 L | 23×13×7 |
| Round Layer Cake Pan | 8×1½ | 1.2 L | 20×4 |
| | 9×1½ | 1.5 L | 23×4 |
| Pie Plate | 8×1¼ | 750 mL | 20×3 |
| | 9×1¼ | 1 L | 23×3 |
| Baking Dish or Casserole | 1 quart | 1 L | — |
| | 1½ quarts | 1.5 L | — |
| | 2 quarts | 2 L | — |